CLERICAL ERRORS

BY

JOHN FEARN

2006.

Published 2005 by arima publishing

www.arimapublishing.com

ISBN 1-84549-058-4

Printed and bound in the United Kingdom

Typeset in Garamond 11/14

arima publishing
ASK House, Northgate Avenue
Bury St Edmunds, Suffolk IP32 6BB
t: (+44) 01284 700321

www.arimapublishing.com

Introduction

It all started, I suppose in 1950. I never dreamt, when I was sixteen years old, that I would end up as a clergyman in the Church of England.. My father wanted me to follow him into his profession as a teacher; my mother wanted me to take up a lucrative career. I had an analytical brain, and being good with my hands, I assumed I would become some form of engineer. It was at that time that my family moved from Hartlebury in Worcestershire, up to London. My father had recently been appointed as headmaster of the Westminster City School in Palace Street, Victoria, opposite Watney's Brewery.

I had been confirmed in 1949 whilst a pupil at Bromsgrove School by the then Bishop of Worcester, Mervyn Charles Edwards – by reputation the only bishop on the Bench at that time without a degree! This was to be a great encouragement to me when I trained, at a later stage, for the ministry.

At school, I was prepared for confirmation along with all those of the same age in my year – it hadn't meant a lot to me at the time, I must admit – it was just something that was 'done' at that certain age. I have only one memory of the Confirmation Service; I was in the school choir at the time – and I remember well the persistent Red Admiral butterfly that hovered, for most of the service, over the choir and the Bishop's head!

Chapter 1

LONDON – 1950 - 1953

I cannot remember exactly how it was that I came to get involved with St. Stephen's Church, Rochester Row – it was probably because I had only recently been confirmed, and was still 'filled with enthusiasm and zeal for the Lord'. I joined a very active local Church Youth Club. This was my first awakening and growing awareness of members of the opposite sex. This set of circumstances [an association with the church and a developing spirituality, not the awareness of the opposite sex!] led eventually to my being ordained in Worcester Cathedral, some eleven years later. Whilst in London, I joined the congregation of St. Stephen's, and before very long, I found myself in the Choir; I became a bell-ringer, which was to be a great advantage in my later ministry, and under the guidance and enthusiasm of Eric James, David Loake and John Chisholm, the then curates under the very charismatic Vicar George Reindorp, who subsequently became Bishop of Guildford, I became a 'singing entertainer' to the old folks after Evensong on Sundays, and a Parish Visitor, visiting the tenement flats of Millbank on behalf of the church. "Knock three times in the Name of the Father, the Son and the Holy *Ghost*" (as He was known then) said George Reindorp, at the briefing for parish visitors. "Be bold – remember, you go out in the name of the Lord!"

George Reindorp's charismatic leadership in London was infectious; there was a very successful Youth Club, a Men's Group, and the women of the congregation absolutely *adored* him. Within the catchment of the parish boundaries were both the Westminster and the Westminster Children's Hospitals, so at all the Sunday services and especially at Evensong, there was always present a bevy of senior and junior nursing staff – some in mufti, but many in uniform, who had come straight to church from duty on the wards. It was during this time that I forged my first relationships with two members of the opposite sex – Joyce Grut, a nurse from the Westminster Children's Hospital, and Joan Tuffley from the Westminster Hospital who I believe subsequently joined a Religious Order. However, my love life is the subject of a different story; this is concerned with my journey of faith, from innocent student to retired and somewhat disillusioned senior clergyman. Disillusioned with the church, I hasten to add, not my faith.

Without doubt, I was inspired and influenced by the incumbent's charisma and down-to-earth sermons, and the fervour of his curates. They were zealous, hard working, deeply spiritual, enthusiastic and welcoming. Few actual memories remain, but I do remember the crowd of parishioners gathered on the platform at Euston Station, when John Chisolm, the senior curate, answered the call to become a missionary in Papua, New Guinea - now Melanesia. It seemed as if more than half the parish had turned up to see him off. Even this had an effect on me. A first taste of what Christian commitment really meant.

The parish also boasted a female Parish Worker – Mavis Salt. She was to figure importantly in my life on the evening that I ended up at the door of her flat, unhappy to the point of distraction with a cry for help, having taken an overdose of aspirins, probably due to a disappointment in an immature love affair, or problems with my parents. I ultimately decided that I didn't want to die after all, and she was my first line of re-course. My parents, to whom I never really related, were horrified – most probably more for the scandal that my action was likely to cause to my father as head of a local private school, and the embarrassment which would reflect on them both, rather than what had brought me to this action. It was George Reindorp who 'arranged' my discreet admission to the Westminster hospital, the 'pumping out' and subsequent return to the bosom of my family!

Called to National Service

I remember little else of relevance during my time in London, other than my various associations with the church. It wasn't long – only a matter of a few years - before I was called up to do my National Service, having been 'deferred' several times, during my time as a student at an Electrical Engineering College. Eventually I failed a set of exams and ended up in Carlisle to do my basic training in the Royal Armoured Corps. I do remember my call-up, and travelling to a draughty Church Hall in North London for a pre-service medical; standing naked and embarrassed in a long line of similar 'draftees' awaiting a series of degrading questions and other medical and intelligence tests. The 'initiation' into 'things military' began with the laborious completion of seemingly endless Army forms by a bored army sergeant whose intelligence would have been challenged by that of an ageing chimpanzee! When we got down to the question 'Religion?' I answered 'Christian' – not to be awkward, but in the interests of accuracy. To this answer, I received the not-too-polite reply "I'll ask you again – what is your religion – C of E, RC or OD? These were the days of virtually no inter-church co-operation, so I had absolutely no idea what 'OD' meant. However, discretion being the better part of valour, I swallowed my pride and my contempt for his lack of religious understanding, and meekly replied, 'Church of England'. I didn't dare make the distinction between 'religion' and 'denomination'. 'OD.' apparently meant 'Other [Christian] Denomination' – there seemed to be little option for Jews, Muslims, Infidels or heretics!! A newly made 'friend' of mine at the selection day did try and say 'agnostic', and he was treated in the same, off-hand manner by the selection sergeant who, not being sure what 'agnostic' meant put him down as 'C of E'.

As these were the days before widespread immigration, any 'ethnic' call-up was unlikely in the extreme. The selection process ended with an 'aptitude' test which was so easy that even a blindfolded chimpanzee could have passed with flying colours; one or two of the lads present were found unfit for duty, both on medical and intellectual grounds. I remember we were asked what regiment we felt we would be most suited for – I opted for the R.E.M.E. in the light of my three years electrical engineering training; however, with the army's typical penchant for mis-management, I was allocated to a Cavalry regiment. I suppose I was lucky that I didn't end up in the Catering Corps – and so were those for whom I might subsequently have been required to cook meals. I remember taking a copy of the latest edition of the local Parish Magazine with me on the train to Carlisle, only to be cautioned by my mother who had come to see me off, who suggested that anyone seeing me would think me a cissy! Perhaps I should have shocked her with a copy of Men Only!

Chapter 2

CARLISLE – 1953

The camp chapel at Carlisle was dreary, as must have been the camp Padre, because I remember hardly anything about it or him at all. I don't even remember 'going to chapel' on a Sunday, though I suppose I must have done – 8 a.m. Holy Communion - to the derision of the rest of my barrack room. My early memory of those days was boots being thrown at a more extrovert evangelical 'born again' Christian in my recruits' squad, who determinedly knelt at his bedside to say his prayers for the first few nights. He finally decided that, in the interests of self-preservation, he would resign himself to saying them silently once he was tucked up in bed.

These were hard days – with the physical training, the assault course and the drill parades; by comparison, the technical and regimental training was a relative doddle. But, despite the rigours of the life, I really enjoyed it. After the initial five weeks of basic instruction, we were allowed a 48-hour leave pass, and then it was back to Hadrian's Camp for trade training. Being an Armoured Car Training Camp, the trades on offer were Armoured Vehicle driving, or Wireless Operator / Gunnery. I chose the latter.

During this second period at Carlisle, I was selected as a 'Potential Officer' – which really only consisted of an extended training programme of Regimental History and Leadership. Following my interview with the CO and his cronies, at which I was asked about my parentage, my finances and whether I saw myself as a long service, regular Officer, I was 'returned to the ranks' – obviously I did not have the necessary 'plum in the mouth' nor a sufficient bank balance to become a cavalry officer!

And so followed trade training in wireless telegraphy, which I passed with flying colours, and gunnery on the ranges which was followed by embarkation leave – and then off to Malaya – aboard if my memory serves me right, the SS 'City of Hongkong'. We disembarked at Singapore, and, after a few days in a holding camp on the island (strains of 'The Virgin Soldiers') my troop travelled by train up to Seremban in Negri Sembilan. By now I was a fully-fledged (but not yet fully acclimatised) wireless operator/gunner on a GMC. (Armoured General Motor Carrier). I do remember we did have a very loud-mouthed bully – a Geordie as one of our two 'in-transit' lance-corporals – a man of very low intelligence whose fists were the answer to any and every problem. It was my first introduction to the rougher side of life!

Chapter 3

SEREMBAN, MALAYA – 1954 – 1956

The practice of religion in a 'front line' army war theatre was very much a low priority activity; I know I have a poor memory, but I remember virtually nothing of the camp chapel at Seremban, nor again of the padre or of any Sunday services. My only memory was of the listing on weekly Regimental Orders of those designated to attend the weekly church parades, and the persuasion [and bribery – a tin of fifty cigarettes] which I was regularly offered for a 'Sunday Service swap' among those who recognised that I was a regular attender, rota or not, and whose preferred occupation on a Sunday was a 'lie-in'. Although it was allowed for men to 'stand in' for others quite legally to provide the Padre with a congregation to preach to, I'm afraid that I declined, happy to watch my roommates squirm with their subsequent obligation to attend 'Army' Matins!

Photo Taken at Paroi Camp, Malaya whilst serving with the 11th Hussars P.A.O.

St. Mark's Church - Seremban

Such was my growing sense of spirituality and spiritual needs however, that I developed the habit of travelling into the Malay town of Seremban to attend the Anglican Communion Service at the local Church of St. Mark. The parish priest was a bi-lingual Tamil Indian, the Reverend George Savarimurthu. He had, as I remember, a Chinese curate at that time. One unique feature of the Sunday Services was the once-a-month (or was it only at festivals?) occasion, when the church held a synchronous celebration of Holy Communion, at the main and two side altars, in three separate languages at the same time – a service I attended and remember with delight. The service was in English at the north aisle altar, in Tamil at the high altar, and in one of the Chinese dialects in the south aisle. The whole event was well choreographed, with each service reaching the consecration and the elevation of the elements (quite 'high' church even in those days!) at exactly the same moment. The Holy Communion was administered at communion rails running right across the church, with no regard for position, race or language.

Ceremonial uniform of the 'Guard of Honour' for the visit of Sir Anthony Eden.

This situation – of attending St Mark's in Seremban most Sundays and in the camp chapel when 'on the rota', continued right through the time I was stationed at Paroi camp. It had fringe benefits; it gave me access to a social life within the local church, which my fellow soldiers were denied – the monthly dances and other socialising, with both English and Eurasian girls. The other ranks relied for their entertainment on the companionship of the 'dance hostesses' at the local bars and dance halls, for which they bought tickets by the book, occasionally meeting up with their hostesses for extra-mural (and extra-marital!) activities as occasion permitted and the troops required.

Out in the jungle - on Detachment

During this period of 'active' service, our troop of Daimler armoured cars and Saracen armoured personnel carriers (by then we had replaced the GMC's) – went on detachment to a camp in the jungle. It was a basic life under canvas, with daily patrols along the jungle roads, sometimes looking for traces of communist terrorist occupation of the villages, and on other occasions escorting food convoys through the hazardous jungle, to prevent the goods they carried being hijacked by the terrorists.

It was the monsoon season, and many of the roads were flooded. So we had an additional duty – to travel daily to the edge of the flooding, and report over the radio its day-to-day location, whether for the better or for the worse. On one occasion that is etched in my memory for evermore, we had stopped at the edge of the flood, which was running furiously over the road on a causeway in open territory, with jungle either side. We were standing by our vehicles, having a 'smoke break' before returning. That day, we were commanded by our troop Sergeant, a good, kind and sensible NCO. As we took our break, two further vehicles from another, infantry detachment arrived at the scene, a five-ton lorry and a fifteen-hundred-weight truck. Our troop sergeant, with considerable experience of both the roads and the depth of flooding, suggested to the staff-sergeant in charge of the other unit that it would *not* be safe to continue further. It was obvious that the staff sergeant held the cavalry regiment in low regard – perhaps he had an inferiority complex. Whatever the reason, he ordered his detachment forward. Again our troop sergeant advised against such a move. The five-tonner was full of supplies, the fifteen-hundredweight contained privates – a few British, but mostly Malay. The Staff Sergeant sent the fifteen-hundredweight lorry through first. It hadn't gone more than fifty yards before it was swept off the road with the pressure of the currents raging over the embankment. As it tumbled over into the flood waters, all we could do was to stand helplessly by and watch between ten and fifteen soldiers drown. They came out of the truck as it tumbled over, and were taken by the flood waters into the mess of jungle scrub and muddy torrents of the surging river. It was my first ever experience of death – and it has remained as vivid as the day it happened, ever since. I never did find out the consequences, though no doubt our troop sergeant was eventually called to give evidence against the folly of that particular infantry Staff

Sergeant.

On another occasion, we had gone out on patrol to visit a 'front-line' detachment – the details now are somewhat hazy – but I do remember sitting at the radio set of my Saracen whilst our troop commander (a senior NCO) and other members of my 'crew' went to fraternise with the men on detachment. Suddenly, there was the sound of a shot – and then another - quite close at hand. Not knowing quite what to expect, but fearing the worst, I reached for my rifle. Suddenly, rushing up to the armoured car came one of the troop with a message from the troop commander, requesting me to put in a call to base from 'Sunray Minor' – the NCO troop commander – requesting medical aid; it was only then that I found out that one of the men on detachment had, rather embarrassingly, shot himself in the buttocks, twice, with his own sten gun!!

Back at Paroi Camp

Some months later, whilst I was stationed at Paroi Camp, I was transferred from the duties of Wireless Operator/Gunner in an active squadron, to that of Transport clerk in HQ Squadron, taking on overall responsibility for the deployment of all the armoured and supply vehicles of the two squadrons used on the camp. Cavalry regiments – (those employing tanks and armoured cars) - have always utilised the anomalous terminology 'troop' and 'squadron', where infantry regiments used the more familiar terms 'squad' and 'platoon'. This is a left over from the equestrian days.

Another memorable event of this time was an excitement for some, and a shock for others. We had an AOP [Air Observation Post] Flight and airstrip on out camp, and a flight of small Auster aeroplanes. We also were visited occasionally by helicopters – and on this occasion a helicopter came onto the runway bearing the dead bodies of three terrorists - two male and one female. It was my first introduction to a mutilated body – previously I had only witnessed my grandparents, laid out to rest in their coffins. How ugly, how sad to witness the ravages of war.

It was during this time that the second major event occurred that was to prove of great significance in my journey towards full time ministry. Army units in the Far East used to circulate each other with details of Courses and 'optional postings' that became available from time to time in other units. In 1955, one of these was the invitation for regiments serving abroad to make known the need for a Film Projectionist / Barman at the School of Religious Instruction, a post situated on the island of Pulau *(Island)* Blakang Mati, a mile or so off the main island of Singapore. With my religious leanings at that time, and with the privilege of being aware of all inter-unit circulars that came into the office, I applied for and got the transfer.

Chapter 4

PULAU BLAKANG MATI, SINGAPORE – 1955

There are those who would argue that by comparison to my previous exploits, it was a 'cushy' posting. There was certainly no 'bull' – but as an NCO working in the 'HQ' offices at Seremban, and 'excused boots' on medical grounds for an ingrowing toenail, life had not involved an excess of 'spit and polish' during my stay there. After all, we were on 'active service'. But down on Blakang Mati Island, life was even easier. My Commanding Officer was a kind and gentle Major in the RAChD (Royal Army Chaplain's Department), and we were a staff of three - an Admin. Sergeant, an army driver and myself along with a staff of native servants. My official responsibilities were running the small bar – something with which I was, up until that time totally unfamiliar, and being the unit's film projectionist. I had better explain. The 'School of Religious Instruction' [SRI for short] was a training centre which ran mid-week, three and four day religious and moral leadership courses for up to 15 to 20 army and air-force personnel, graded by rank and sex. There were courses for 'other ranks' – for junior and senior NCO's (not together!) junior and senior officers (again, not together), and for WRAC and WRAF other ranks, women NCO's and officers. It all sounds very technical, but with the army's penchant for dividing the classes, ranks and sexes, it all made perfect sense – to them at least!

An embarrassing moment.

The courses, rather along the lines of 'Confirmation Preparation' – and some of them were just that, comprised lectures, discussion groups, with free time for recreation in the afternoons (reading, walking, or just sleeping!) - and in the evenings, further talks, discussions and film shows. I had been up to Kuala Lumpur on a film projectionists' course – so on my return, using an old Bell & Howell 16mm projector, and a set of appropriate biblical, moral and religious films, I would show these through the window of the conference room - the 'throw' of the projector lens being too long for me to be in the same room as the audience. Warm sea breezes meant that the audience (or certain members of it) occasionally dropped off to sleep. I well remember one occasion when, after a particularly busy week, with a course of senior officers who for three or four days had eaten and drunk well – keeping me up into the early hours of each morning serving them from the bar (the other of my official responsibilities) - that, at the evening film show on the fifth night, I nearly achieved a court martial! It was a warm, balmy evening. I was tired. I was showing a two-reel, full-length film – 3200 ft. The film was running smoothly – I had seen it a dozen times or more before. Half way through the first reel, I dropped off to sleep. After the projector had run to the end of the first reel, the senior officers waited patiently for the new reel to be threaded. Nothing happened. They were very patient. Eventually one of them came out to find out what was amiss. Not only was I asleep, but to make matters worse, ,the take up spool had jammed, and I was faced with some 1200 feet of film, all in a pile, in the monsoon drain outside the conference room. The senior officers were very kind – they recognised how tired they had made me during a week of late drinking, and nothing further was said; I managed to re-wind the film, free of damage.

We had a delightful chapel on site even though it was only a converted Nissen hut; it was used for Sunday worship and devotional talks, taken by the Padre – Mark Green, who after leaving the forces, eventually became Suffragan Bishop of Aston in Birmingham. The chapel had no regular pianist, but it did have an old, pedal harmonium. I had been taught by a Danish girlfriend to play the piano by ear, having given up whilst a boy what I considered to be boring piano lessons and interminable practice! How I regretted that action in my later years. I was recruited to play the hymns for weekday and occasional Sunday services, and I also sang in the choir at the local Garrison church. I had a limited repertoire of hymns – limited only by those that could be played and sung in F# major - the only key in which I could play!! However, I managed – and I enjoyed life on the island – the camaraderie, the job and the surroundings. I was allowed the use of the padre's auto-cycle to go down to the village shops, and there was also an island bus that visited on an irregular basis.

I have only three further memories of my time on Blakang Mati – one, an occasion of great mischief which earned me (and the camp driver) a serious reprimand – and another concerning the loss of my virginity – (I really was a 'virgin' soldier in those days!) both of which are detailed in another book – and a third, an occasion of deep spiritual influence, which I must record, as it again relates to my spiritual journey to ministry.

A day of deep spiritual significance
I had been over to the mainland for some reason or other, and had come back late. Motorised sampans (small motor boats) were available at all hours of the day and night to ferry one to and from the island. But it was well past midnight – I was on legitimate 'time off' – but the prospect of a three-mile walk across the island, in the dark, even along familiar roads was daunting – and all the available taxis were long since gone. I set off. It was a good road, but it meandered through some quite dense jungle, and it was a night of a new moon. Visibility was at a premium. For once in my life I was scared. 'Put one foot in front of the other', I told myself. And then I started to recite, quietly, the words of the twenty-third psalm. "Yea, though I walk through the valley of the shadow of death, I will fear no evil...." Suddenly, at that point, I was aware of a miracle. I felt calm. I felt secure. I felt at peace. I walked the rest of the journey with confidence. God was with me. I had no need to fear. Not that I was likely to be ambushed by communist terrorists, as could so easily have been the case whilst on detachment from Seremban in the Malayan jungle. The island was a 'safe'

island. But I had a fear of the dark, and of the unknown until that night, when I recited the words of the twenty-third psalm.

Padre Mark Green, in the nine months that I was stationed on the island at SRI had had a profound affect on my spiritual life – by his presence, his teaching and his support. I don't even remember if I ever discussed with him any thoughts that I might have had for a future in the ministry – indeed, I don't think that at that stage I had had any particular, or definite leanings towards it. But I am indebted to Mark Green, just as I had been to George Reindorp earlier, for the support and encouragement they gave me during those two distinctly influential periods in my life.

Chapter 5

BACK AT PAROI CAMP, SEREMBAN – 1956

After a nine-month sojourn on Blakang Mati, I returned to my regiment, more convinced than ever that I was being called to ministry. However, for me the call when it came was not a cataclysmic, earth shattering moment – rather a growing realisation that I was not called to be an electrical engineer on completing my National Service. So I decided first to sign on as a regular soldier. This would give me all the time that I needed to think things through, and have the added bonus of increasing my weekly rate of pay. The option in those days was to sign on for '22 years with the Colours' [regiment] – with the option of ending the 'contract' without penalty at the conclusion of any three-year period.

It was about four weeks after my 'change of status' from National Service recruit to regular soldier had become official by being published in Regimental Standing Orders, that I believed I was destined to a life in the Ministry. I applied for an interview with the C.O. I was marched in. I stood at ease. "Well, Corporal, why did you ask to see me?" he asked. "To let you know sir, that although I am happy in the regiment, and have signed on as a regular, I feel I am being called to be a priest in the Church of England. I shall therefore be applying to leave the regiment in three years time when my period of service comes up for review." "Don't be such a bloody fool" was the reply, "you've got a good career in the regiment in front of you!" The C.O. did everything in his power to convince me otherwise, which only made me the more determined to follow the convictions of my heart. I promised a continuing loyalty to the regiment, and zealous and conscientious work for the army in the time that remained, and was marched out. I felt calm. I just knew I had done what had to be done, although the enormity of what lay ahead was just a dream. What did I do when I was de-mobbed? Where did I go? Whom did I see? How did I go about offering myself for the ministry? At this point, I think I may have had recourse to the camp Chaplain, though scant memory of this remains.

Chapter 6

BACK IN THE U.K. – CARLISLE – 1957

I served out my time in Seremban and in due course, came back to the UK with the regiment at the end of their tour of duty. I returned to Hadrian's Camp, Carlisle. Again, I think I must have sought help from the camp padre, but this again is but a vague memory. Whilst I had been in Malaya, my parents had moved from Westminster to Couldson in Surrey, and I do vaguely remember, whilst on leave, asking advice of the local Vicar. He advised me to contact CACTM (The Churches Advisory Council for the Ministry), which I did. Not being particularly impressed with Sunday services at the camp chapel, I attached myself instead to a church on the edge of Carlisle – by strange co-incidence, a sister church to my church in London, also dedicated to St. Stephen, and under the same patronage, Lady Angela Burdett-Coutts. [It is sad to have to relate that when I re-visited Carlisle many years later in the 1970's, both Army camp and church had been demolished to make way for new developments – a motor-way by-pass and new housing on the site of the old camp, and a petrol station (ironically named St. Stephen's Garage!) on the site of the original church] Whilst a member of St. Stephen's, I was befriended by the then Vicar and his wife, the Revd. John and Mrs. Davidson, with whom I spent most Sundays – attending Morning Service, having lunch and tea at the Vicarage and then going again to Evensong with them before returning to camp. The Davidson family, including, as I remember now, an 'adopted' daughter from a north European country, were kindness personified.

The first steps towards Ministry
Whilst still working out my days in the army, I got leave to go on a selection conference. Twenty-three of us were there, from all walks of life. There were four interviewers – and formal and informal interviews were held at any time of the day for three long days. We conversed with our interviewers one-at-a-time, in groups, during meals (we rotated the seating plan) and during cosy walks in the grounds of Bagshot Park in Surrey. They discovered through their interrogations that I did not even have an 'O' level pass in Divinity - as it was called at school at that time – or Religious Knowledge as it is more familiarly known. It was apparently a pre-requisite of consideration for ordination! The result? I was given a 'provisional' acceptance, on the condition of a successful future passing of the 'O' level exam. I was among about five that were provisionally accepted for one academic condition or another – three were 'not recommended' – the others got through unhindered. But no one normally knew what the 'pass' rate was; it was never published. So in one of our few moments of corporate privacy, we engineered a scheme to break the system. I had

duplicating facilities available in my father's school office. So I offered to be the co-ordinator. When each candidate received their 'result', they sent it to me; I co-ordinated them, and sent them back out again to each member of the group. This is how we found out about the pass / fail rate, although even those that 'failed' or were 'not recommended' were invited to try again at a later date.

And so I set about achieving this goal. I studied using a correspondence course, and eventually entered myself for the 'O' level exam through a local secondary school in Carlisle. I well remember the embarrassment of sitting the exam in the gymnasium, among some two hundred children and three nuns. They were in their habits and I was in uniform. It was a bizarre situation. We stuck out like sore thumbs among all those children, but I passed the exam. Another hurdle achieved towards my goal.

It was round about this time that I was 'adopted' by the Davidson family at St. Stephen's in Carlisle. I had joined the choir at the church, and having been selected by CACTM for training for the ministry, I was then offered the unique opportunity of preaching in the church at Evensong one Sunday. I have never been so nervous in my life! I suppose I had always had a streak of unconventionality in my bones, so, instead of starting off in a familiar Anglican way, with the words, "I take my text from..." I decided to be different. When the congregation had settled in their seats (and for some reason, half the nave lights had been extinguished to save electricity, though it was conducive to those in the back row dropping off to sleep) – I began, and some of the congregation looked up in alarm. "Where are we going?" asked Piglet. "Anywhere", said Pooh. So off they went together...." It was sermon centred on the direction of a Christian's life, and having always had an affinity with the works of A. A. Milne, I couldn't resist the temptation of starting my sermon in this unconventional way. I remember the Vicar in the vestry after the service complimenting me on my delivery, but adding, somewhat ruefully, "It was a bit of an unusual beginning, though!"

Chapter 7

DURHAM – THE BERNARD GILPIN SOCIETY – 1958

Having passed my GCSE in Religious Knowledge, and so fulfilled the necessary conditions, now came the serious business of choosing a theological college. It was a steep learning curve. I was naive – I was unaware of the distinctions within the Church of England – Anglo-Catholic, Middle of the Road and Evangelical – or, in the common parlance of ordinands of the time, Spiky, Broad and Rock-Bottom-Protestant [North End 'Rock-Bot-Prot'!] So where did I fit into the scheme of things? I had been brought up being used to vestments, probably due to my father's influence. My mother though came from a Welsh Baptist background – this contradiction between my parents had been a regular source of aggravation to my father who was intolerant of any religious observance other than his own. They had been married in St. Cybi's Episcopal Church in Holyhead, despite the fact that my maternal grandfather was a convinced Welsh Baptist and a lay preacher to boot! I had learnt quite a bit about the differences in churchmanship during my selection conference; I was to learn more during a pre-theological year that I was required to serve at a 'gathered College' created by CACTM for those, like myself, who had been out of academic training for a while – in the forces, in industry, or wherever. This 'college' - for that is what we were, was based in a teetotal hotel in Durham, and we took our name from Bernard Gilpin, deemed the 'Apostle of the North' during his ministry in County Durham. We were granted all the opportunities that the university had to offer in the way of libraries, extra-mural lectures and other facilities. We were allocated two members of staff – a principal, Bernard Jacob and a Tutor, John [JSC] Abrahams. Alongside the nineteen of us 'potential ordinands' were four other trainees for full time work with the Y.M.C.A. We were a motley bunch – of all aspirations – some 'holy joes', attending daily Mass in the high church parish churches of the town, and some evangelicals, who needed no church building, but prayed 'in the Spirit' in one of the lounges of the hotel – the phenomenon and practice of which I was totally unfamiliar, due to my somewhat closeted upbringing. The outcome of this 'coming together' of the various strands of Anglican churchmanship meant that, for Sunday worship we attached ourselves to the various parish churches of the city; the evangelicals to St. Nicholas in the market place, and the anglo-catholic element to St. Oswald's on the outskirts of the city. The vicar of this church, the Revd. Kenneth Meux and his wife were very kind and welcoming to us 'high church' students, and we, in our turn did what we could for the parish, assisting with their summer fete, and generally taking part in the general life of the church. During the week, a regular group of us used to attend Holy Communion at Durham Cathedral –

two favourites of mine were St. Chad's chapel at the west end of the building, and the chapel of the Nine-altars at the east end. We were nearly late for breakfast one morning when the celebrant, well past retirement age got into a time warp, and started repeating a cycle of the service over and over again! It was only the unison chorus of loud, emphatic students that finally unhitched him from repeating himself into perpetuity!

Contact with the University

We were in Durham for three terms only – from the September to the following June. As well as our academic studies, we managed to integrate into the social life of the various parish churches, and the life of the university. Durham is unique in that it had two theological colleges – St. Chad's for high church students, and St. John's for the evangelicals. It was alleged that, on the occasion of a visiting prelate to St. John's to deliver a sermon, members of St. Chad's college 'acquired' a road sign which they placed just outside the college chapel door. It read, "Don't Cross Here!"

Our greatest non-academic achievement as an 'up-start' college during our time in Durham was to win the annual shield in the University Rag Week procession of floats, beating all the regular colleges into first place, despite their prolific resources. They were not amused!

During this time we learnt a lot about each other, and the varying Christian traditions from which we had come. It was a time of growing together in understanding and mutual respect. I made three good friends at this time; three of us went on together to Lichfield to further our training, considered one of the 'Higher' Anglo-Catholic theological colleges; George Buckler, the 'fourth musketeer' went to Oakhill, an evangelical college of fundamentalist teaching and practice. But our friendships had been forged – and we never lost the camaraderie of that first significant year.

One benefit for me of this period in Durham was the opportunity of learning about the various College options available, and where best to make my applications. Financially I had no savings or reserves. I relied totally on grants; my parents, who had spent considerable sums during my electrical engineering training at Faraday House in London, were no longer prepared to support me in my new quest, apart from free 'hospitality' during the college vacations. During these periods, I was obliged to find temporary work, to help me fund non-administrative costs during term time – books, and the costs of maintaining my transport of the time – a second-hand 125 c.c. BSA Bantam motorcycle. I had a wide diversity of work; typist to a detective fiction-writing parson, secretary to the administrator of the Ballet Rambert, and shoe salesman at the School Outfitters, Daniel Neal's in Oxford Street. At least it kept the wolf from the door, provided petrol for my motorcycle, and theological textbooks for my studies.

Chapter 8

LICHFIELD THEOLOGICAL COLLEGE
1959 – 1961

Members of Lichfield Theological College leaving the Cathedral after singing Evensong.

College days were good days; the work was hard, especially learning New Testament Greek; I was relieved not to have had to learn Hebrew as well! The regular pattern was four services a day, starting with Matins and Holy Communion first thing in the morning; Sext at mid-day; Evensong just before dinner, and Compline before bedtime. Then it was back to our rooms for some serious studying, essay writing and note transcribing. As students we took it in turns to act as sacristans (preparing the vestments and altar) serving at Communion, and taking the non-eucharistic services, two days at a time. During these periods, it was an added responsibility to sit next to the college principal at meals. I well remember one fateful day when I had just officiated at Evensong; we trooped into the refectory and took our places, waiting for the college staff to enter, and grace to be said. The staff came in; a silence descended on all those present, and the Principal, John Fenton, on taking his place, leaned over towards me, and sotto voce (but in a voice I am sure he *knew* would be heard by all those present), said, "The King is *Dead*!!" The whole room erupted. I hadn't noticed, but having used an ancient prayer book for taking the service in the chapel, I had inadvertently prayed for 'King George the Sixth and all the Royal Family'!!

We studied, we attended lectures and talks from visiting speakers; I well remember the eponymous Nicholas Stacey, who shocked us all with his suggestion that Lichfield Cathedral just the other side of the road from our college was obsolete, and should be turned into a bus garage. An indignant student criticised his 'lack of respect for tradition and architecture', to which he replied, "I couldn't care a fish's tit"!! We were learning, the hard way, to accept that not everyone thought, or behaved quite as we did. One of my glorious memories was singing a late night, plainsong service of Compline on a Good Friday night in the Lady Chapel of St. Chad's Cathedral, a poignant memory that has remained with me ever since.

A call from the Blood Transfusion Service
My other vivid memory of my time in Lichfield is a sad one. John Fenton's wife, Mary, who was like a mother to us in times of stress and need, contracted cancer. For many months she was kept alive with regular blood transfusions. As her life ebbed away, I was part of a week long, twenty-four-hour-a-day prayer vigil for her. She died. We performed the music for her funeral in the cathedral. She was cremated, and her remains were buried in the cathedral close. As a blood donor (I had been 'enlisted' whilst in the army just prior to demobilisation), I had been trying to encourage my fellow students to enrol, but with scant success. Some weeks following Mary's death, the N.B.T.S. (National Blood Transfusion Service as it was then) arranged a further visit to Lichfield. I advertised the visit. The college students, almost to a man, turned up at the session. I was astounded. I was proud. I was humbled. I was grateful. I was delighted.

Our social life was somewhat masculine based, although we did, during the summer months, arrange several tennis matches against the girls of the sixth form of the nearby Girls' school. But, on the whole, it was a fairly monastic existence; the regime had originally been set up by the former principal, a Dr. Hann, by whom I was interviewed for a place at the college; by the time I arrived, he had left to join the Roman Catholic Church, and he had been replaced by John Fenton, a much more moderate, but eminently qualified New Testament theologian.

The development of Liturgy and music
These were the days of developing change in the church's liturgy. By comparison to the wider-reaching changes in the church of the present day, our alterations to the services were somewhat modest. However, within the realms of music, these were the halcyon days of the 'Twentieth Century Church Light Music Group', among whose members were Patrick Appleford, with the avant-garde new words and music of 'Lord Jesus Christ, you have come to us...', Geoffrey Beaumont, famous for his setting of the Eucharist – the 'Beaumont Mass' which had added the new hymn 'Christ our King in glory reigning...' and the catchy tune for the confirmation hymn, 'O Jesus I have promised...' The Revd. Cyril Taylor had produced his exciting new tune for the well known hymn, 'Glorious things of Thee are spoken', and Michael Brierley, a student

contemporary of ours at college, who wrote several new tunes to some of the more popular hymns, notably, 'At the Name of Jesus...'. He used us as guinea-pigs. So many of his new hymns and tunes were tried out first in the college chapel, though I must repeat that these were conservative days in the church. It was much easier to get away with writing new tunes to familiar words; in all, the Group wrote eighty new tunes to existing hymns. Congregations were far less willing to adopt new words, new thinking and up-dated theological expression. Even the concept of 'You' and 'Yours' for 'Thee' and 'Thine' was anathema to many! [And to some it is still!]

With my Father, Mother and Sister following my ordination as deacon in Worcester Cathedral.

Four terms a year, staying in college for the festivals of Easter and Christmas, and examinations – twelve in all – in four sets of three. As I said, the work was hard, but I passed. Even my father, who came from a long line of schoolmasters was a little surprised. I think that secretly he had always hoped that I would follow him into the teaching profession. However, my 'modernist, theological outlook', gained under the influence of John Fenton did not amuse him in the slightest. The more I tried to explain what I thought and felt, the more the shutters went up, and the more he retreated behind his Anglo-catholic defences.

With the Clergy, Choir. Organist and Churchwardens outside St. Stephen's Church, Redditch – My first Curacy.

Chapter 9

REDDITCH - ST. STEPHEN'S CHURCH
1961 - 1964

The next hurdle to be faced in the pursuit of ministry was finding a suitable parish in which to 'serve my title', as a Deacon for a year, before becoming a fully-fledged priest. And here again was a difficulty. All my college friends and colleagues, having been England-based all their lives, knew clergy, knew Archdeacons and knew Bishops. They knew what they wanted, and where they wanted to go. I, by comparison, was still naive in that respect. Who should I contact? Where should I offer myself?

John Fenton recommended that I wrote, in the first instance to the Bishop of Birmingham, who at that time was the heroic Rt. Revd. Leonard Wilson, whom I held in great awe. He it was who had been imprisoned in Changi jail in Singapore, during the time of the Japanese occupation, and who had proved such an inspiration to his fellow prisoners. However, as it turned out, a job in the Birmingham diocese was not to be, and so I was recommended to the then Bishop of Worcester, Mervyn Charles Edwards. He offered me the post of junior curate in the parish of St. Stephen's, Redditch, a parish which included a large Council housing estate with its own re-inforced concrete dual purpose building, a combination church and hall, at Batchley. There were four of us on the staff - Douglas Rowe, the Vicar, William Paice, senior curate, Gwen Gittins, a lay Parish Worker and myself. Accommodation was found for me, and on the 28th May 1961, I was ordained in Worcester Cathedral. Sadly, I remember little of the ordination service itself – I imagine I held the same feelings for the 'occasion' as a bride on her wedding day, with the atmosphere and sense of occasion seeming so unreal as to make one almost unaware of what was happening around. I did make the vows, though, and I was ordained – or more accurately 'made Deacon' - of that I am sure!

The early days after ordination
I was 'billeted' initially in the house of a parishioner - who seldom if ever went to church, and whose sole claim on my memory was shouting at his little dog – making him sit *'on this very spot'* at every available opportunity. The dog didn't seem to enjoy the shouting all that much. Neither did I. I remember so well my first day 'in the parish', in my dog collar.

I was a fairly heavy smoker – a habit I'd acquired out in Malaya, when Lord Nuffield, out of his misplaced generosity, had paid for every serving soldier to be given free of charge, 50 cigarettes a week. With a friend giving you their ration for a nominal sum, and the army price in the NAAFI only about 1/6d for 50, I came back to England a regular smoker on about 20 a day. As I say – I was in the parish, in my dog collar, and I had run out of cigarettes. My collar and calling impinged on my conscience – "Could I honestly go into a tobacconist's shop and buy the dreadful weed?" It took a while to gather up courage – but I did, and after that first time, it became easier!

My next memory was the occasion of my first 'Parish Garden Party'. It was an Indian summer, and we were all sweltering. I decided to be unconventional. I wore dark grey trousers, and a clean white shirt, with my stock (the black bit) and my clerical collar inside the neck of my white shirt. As I did not own a beige linen summer jacket (in which my vicar was attired) I thought it would be a perfectly acceptable summer alternative. The Vicar wasn't so sure – but there I was, mingling with the crowd – I got away with it! I suppose, looking back, this was the first occasion during my ministry when I broke with tradition – and I have been doing it, more or less, on and off, ever since.

I was ordained Priest just over a year later, on the 17th June 1962, at St. Stephen's Parish Church, Barbourne in Worcester. It was a great disappointment to me not to be ordained priest in Worcester Cathedral, but these were the days when the church was beginning to move away from the formal confines of the cathedral, and out into the parish churches. I must admit that I was a mite jealous of the curate whose church, St. Stephen's, just happened to be where he was serving his diaconate.

During this second year, I met and married Jill, a local Primary School teacher. It was common knowledge (and a bit of a joke, too) among junior clergy that the options for marriageable partners for clergy were confined to nurses and teachers, these being the two groups of females with whom we came most into regular contact. And it proved to be the case. We were married in August 1962, by which time I had moved from my first digs, and the second ones too, and was living temporarily at the Vicarage. But marriage gave me the entitlement to free married accommodation, rather like in the army. Not that this was the reason for my marriage – but there was a curate's house available, and into it we moved. A little Victorian end-of-terrace house, within spitting distance of the Parish Church; here it was that Rebecca, our first child was born. Meanwhile, the 'trivial round, the common task' of Sunday and weekday services continued, with the four of us on the staff taking one day a week as a day off. My day-off was Monday, the same as the Vicar's. I had made friends with some of the younger members of the congregation. I was invited to play tennis... ...on a Saturday! I recollect going, cap in hand to the Vicar, to ask nervously if I could change my day off. Reluctantly as it seemed, he agreed. These were my naive, early days in ministry.

A brush with the 'Establishment'

As junior curate, one of my responsibilities, along with the other members of the parish 'staff' was to attend on rota, the Friday evening 'Vestry Open' evenings, when two members of the parish 'team' made themselves available in St. Stephen's Church vestry for an hour or so, for three main purposes. Firstly, we were available to conduct the Service of 'Churching' – for new young mothers following the birth of a baby. We were also there to issue Certificates of Banns following their reading of the banns for three weeks in church, to make initial arrangements for the many weddings to be held at the parish church, and to arrange baptisms. These latter arrangements usually followed directly on from the Churching Service. There was a lot of superstition in the Midlands about what a new mother could or could not do before she was 'churched' – often she was not allowed over the threshold of her parents' or in-laws' doorstep, following the Old Testament concept of the association of 'child-birth' with 'uncleanness'. So the Friday night ritual was urgent and important, though it should be remembered that, as distinct from the theology of the Old Testament, the Church's view was very different – a 'Service of Thanksgiving' for the Birth of a Child.' It also was a good point of contact for bereavement counselling on those sad occasions which followed a still-born baby. My Vicar insisted that, immediately following the service (normally held at the altar rail of the Lady Chapel), we should hold out an offertory bag for the 'thanksgiving offerings' of the young mother. Many of our 'clients' were not well off; I felt that the more discreet practice would be to leave the bag on the altar rail, and make mention of it before leaving the chapel.

Unfortunately, my Vicar eventually caught me out in this discrete practice, and reprimanded me for not complying with his directions. So, on the next occasion, I 'held out the bag' – and the young girl, embarrassed, put a pound note in it. I took it back to the vestry, whereupon the Vicar proceeded to put the money straight into his pocket! I remonstrated with him, explaining that I considered that the young mother probably imagined that she was making a donation to the church, not to the Vicar. To this, I received the reply: "It's one of the 'perks' of being a Vicar!" I did not agree. And so I took it upon myself, on a pastoral visit, discreetly to ask the young mother in question where she thought her contribution had gone. "To the Church, of course" she replied! After that, whenever opportunity presented itself, I either conveniently 'forgot' to take a bag out to the Lady Chapel, or invited the suppliants to place an offering in the wall safe at the back of the church on their way out.

Dressed 'in-appropriately' for my first summer 'Parish garden party'!

Chapter 10

REDDITCH - AT BATCHLEY MISSION
1962 – 1964

Outside the Mission at Batchley – St. David's Church – with members of the Choir.

During my year as a deacon, I received a wonderful piece of good fortune. The senior curate was offered a new parish. Up until then, he had had almost sole charge of the daughter (Mission) church at Batchley on the council estate, on the outskirts of the parish. He moved out of the parish a week before I was due to be ordained priest. Circumstances necessitated a continuing link between St. David's and the parish church, so, from the moment I was ordained priest, I was given virtual sole responsibility for the congregation at Batchley. Promotion indeed! Mind you, they were funny folk, and it was only a Nissen Hut dual purpose Mission Church. It wasn't licensed for weddings, and the folk on the estate all wanted to get married in the parish church 'with the proper shaped windows'. They were happy to be buried from St. David's though, and most were happy to have their children baptised there, though some were a little sceptical about the validity of a christening held in a Nissen hut. But it was a good learning curve, and I benefitted from it, especially my first foray into dense, council house habitation. Having had a privileged upbringing, I had never before come into contact with working class families en masse. Until then, I had lived a very sheltered life. Not any more. Two incidents stand out from my time there, working the estate.

Baptism dilemmas

The first was being called to visit a family to arrange the baptism of their latest arrival. I called on the family, and was given a warm welcome. The television was on in the corner – no one thought to turn it off; I carried on regardless. I no longer remember the name of the children in the family. It was a long time ago. But, I got out the requisite form, and took down the details. It was little use asking if the parents, let alone the godparents were confirmed. Some of them weren't even baptised themselves. And I had to deal with some very strange requests for 'Christian' names. Zak, I remember, and Sexton Junior, and Diabolo. There was none of your football or pop-star idols in those days. Anyway – I was just making my farewells, when the mother, who obviously had something on her mind asked, "Can I ask you something?" "Yes" I replied, intrigued. "Would you baptise my second youngest at the same time?" So again I sat down, and took down the details. "Any more", I asked, enquiringly? "Yes" she replied. The fathers were rarely present on these occasions. The outcome was *seven* forms completed, for children ranging from new-born to nineteen! The eldest girl looked most embarrassed, but with a bit of extra persuasion, I convinced her that it wouldn't be at all embarrassing – I wouldn't be picking *her* up and holding her over the font!

Crime and the Church

The other 'happening' concerned a theft from the church. Being unaware of the need for tight security on the premises in those days, I had set up a 'pile of pennies' in the church, to raise funds for repairs to the church building, after the manner of the public houses of the time. A circle of twelve pennies, soaked in beer to give them sticking power, and then each layer placed alternately over the previous coins, to give the whole structure strength. It must have reached a height of some fourteen inches – in value about £7 in old money – and, one night, the church was broken into, and the pennies stolen. I reported the theft to the police, only to be remonstrated with for putting such a temptation in the way of the local scallywags. The police didn't hold out much hope for an arrest, let alone a conviction. "Probably only children, anyway" they said.

Two days later, my churchwarden's wife was returning from the shops, when one of the local children, no older than five or six, stopped her in the street and asked her if she had any change. When she asked what for, the boy asked, "Have you got a sixpence for the 'phone?" She found a sixpence, offered it to the lad, whereupon he got out a whole handful of dirty pennies, clearly arc-marked with beer, and counted out six! She asked his name and address innocently, reported it to the police, but sadly they were unable to do anything under the law, although the father and the older brothers were all known to be local thieves and rascals. The children responsible had all been under the age of criminal responsibility!

Among my other 'claims to fame' whilst at Redditch was an attempt to bring (drag) the church into the twentieth century. We ran a very successful weekly Youth Club at St. David's, and I was asked if I could arrange a Sunday Service appropriate to young people. In trepidation I put the idea before the Vicar. He granted me leave to go ahead, but made it quite clear that it really wasn't his scene. So Redditch Parish Church held its first 'Beat' Service, with guitars, drums, the lot! It was hardly a sensation judged by today's standards, but it least it was a move in the right direction.

Liturgical Revision and the 'Established Church'
It was around this time that I attended with Jill, my wife, a symposium at Birmingham University on *'An Experimental Liturgy'*. Liturgy – the 'ordering of worship' - had been a subject that had always fascinated me – it was a particular interest. Ever since my teenage years, I had never been able to understand why Church services never made a lot of sense. In a flashback to my days in London, I can remember accompanying my sister to church, shortly after her confirmation. The service, as I remember it, was recited, sotto voce a 'few miles distant' at the high altar, and I was told firmly to 'stay in my seat' when my sister went up to receive communion. None of it had anything to say to me at all. The keynote speaker at the symposium was an Anglican well ahead of his time – Gilbert Cope, a lecturer in the Department of Extra-Mural Studies at the University of Birmingham. The conference dealt with three main topics – language, symbolism and movement. The question was asked, time and time again, "*Why* do we do this?" More often than not the answer that came back was, "Because we *always have done!*" Nobody, it seemed had questioned the church liturgy at all since 1662. But although it was deemed to be a rite followed 'to the letter' in the majority of Anglican churches, by the time I was ordained and taught to 'celebrate the holy mysteries', several 'adjustments' had become established practice. Others, sadly not! For example, one was expected to recite the Lord's Prayer twice during the service of Holy Communion, once at the beginning, either audibly, or muttered to oneself whilst facing the altar, and then again later in the service, along with the congregation. Gilbert Cope explained that this was only because the first Lord's Prayer was a 'left-over' from the end of the Priest's private service of Preparation from the Latin Mass – however, it had certainly formed no part of the first and second Prayer Books of Edward the Sixth of 1548 and 1552. Again, the 'Summary of the Law' was used

extensively as an alternative to the Ten Commandments, despite the fact that it was illegal – coming as it did from the 'adopted' Prayer Book of 1928. The Collect for the Queen was often omitted, as certainly were the three long 'exhortations', but an 'Agnus Dei' and 'Benedictus' were often inserted, which formed no part of the approved liturgy. The Church was beginning albeit slowly, and illegally, to 'adapt' its worship to the needs of the people. The Experimental Liturgy went several stages further but although the suggested changes seemed dramatic at that time, the one change that even the liturgical reformers weren't bold enough to suggest was the alteration of the accepted text from 'Thee' to 'You'. By the time I was ordained priest, I was still expected to celebrate according to the letter of the Book of Common Prayer of 1662, but with the accepted exceptions!

An introduction to Christian Giving

Another small but significant event was, unwittingly, to colour my outlook on life, and have a profound effect on my later ministry. The parish was desperate for funds – this was long before the days of 'Christian Stewardship' organised on a diocesan basis. The only available solution was to employ an outside 'fund-raiser' – and this is what my then Vicar decided to do. He called in the 'Wells' organisation, a professional funding company who ran campaigns on a very American basis. It was an 'all church member' approach and worked on the system of what I can only term 'revealed pledges'.

The parish staff was called upon to compile a list of all parishioners who had any link whatsoever with the church – however strong, however tenuous. They were then all invited to a 'Campaign Supper', at which, following the meal, speeches were made by significant church members – churchwarden, Treasurer, Organist etc; each table of parishioners was provided with a 'hostess' responsible for visiting the 'clients' and ensuring their presence at the meal, and a 'visitor' who would subsequently visit the family to elicit a pledge. The wealthiest parishioners were visited first, and later, the less financially blessed. Then, when those visited asked, "So, how much are we being invited to give each week?" the answer was readily forthcoming – "Well, *Mr. Smith* has pledged £5 a week…" It was spiritual and financial blackmail; the incumbent was required to stand in the pulpit and reveal his new weekly pledged amount; other influential (and wealthy) parishioners were then required to do likewise, although some were not prepared to participate – the requirement caused a minor rebellion in the parish. The Wells organisation worked on a percentage fee system; if the parish did as they required, they would underwrite and guarantee the total projected sum; in the event, they did come *near* the required figure, but because the parishioners were not 100% co-operative, the agreement was declared null and void. It did, however, get the parish out of financial difficulties, and a weekly envelope giving scheme was set up as a result. During the course of the campaign, even I was visited, and I remember that occasion well. As a parish 'professional', we discussed the campaign; its merits, its likely financial outcome, and my expected giving level. At that meeting, I offered a quite modest, weekly amount. As my 'visitor' was leaving, he just happened to comment, "I notice you smoke!" "Yes", I replied, "it's a habit I developed whilst in the army in Malaya." "So how many cigarettes a week do you smoke?" he asked. "About twenty a day," I replied. "That must be expensive" he said quietly – that'll be costing you about seven times what you're proposing to give to God each week for the work of the church. Goodnight!" And with that he walked away. I stood on the doorstep – totally non-plussed. He was right, of course, and from that moment I was converted to 'Christian' giving.. My offering through the church from that day has since been based proportionately on the amount I spend on myself and my own pleasures. This 'example from life' was to stand me in good stead later in my ministry, but I had little knowledge then of how valuable that little scene enacted on the doorstep was going to prove!

It was during this time that our first daughter, Rebecca was born; the parishioners were delighted, and my wife and daughter eventually became regular worshippers at Morning Service, with a portable car-seat hooked over the back of the pew in front.. However, it must be said that Sung Matins was not the best liturgical vehicle for a small, crying baby, and sadly by this stage in the reforming life of the Church of England, such ideas as 'All Age Family Worship' and 'informal family services' were little more than a distant dream. The only spiritual outlet for young mothers with babies and toddlers was the mid-week afternoon 'Pram Service' – satisfying the spiritual needs of neither children nor their parents.

In due course, a new 'junior' curate was appointed to the parish. I was promoted to 'senior' curate, and life fell into a new pattern. Until, of course, the time also came for me to 'move on'. I began looking for a post of more responsibility, being eternally grateful for the circumstances that had provided me with such a wide experience and such an advantageous start to my ministry.

Chapter 11

BLADON - The Churchill Years 1964 – 1967

St. Martin's Church, Bladon – from the North side.

Because, unlike so many young clergy in the Church of England, I had few contacts with dioceses, their bishops or other clerics, I was forced to use the facilities of the church press to seek a new parish. It was considered very 'de rigeur' in those days; one was supposed to 'put one's name about', so that invitations would come flowing in from all quarters. However, I saw an advertisement in the Church Times seeking a senior Curate for the parish of Bladon with Woodstock in the diocese of Oxford. It would be a unique appointment inasmuch as the curate's post was to service the *parish* church of Bladon – a small village of some thousand parishioners, whilst the Rector, under whom I would be working, was responsible for the church, [more correctly styled the chapel-of-ease] of St. Mary Magdalene, in the market town of Woodstock, within whose parameters lay the stately home of Blenheim Palace, home to the Duke of Marlborough.

Having been for the most part brought up in India until I was eleven years of age, learning Indian History and Indian Geography as a priority, and English

Geography and History as a minor subject, I was totally unaware of the British feudal system and the various ranks of the nobility. So it was that, when I mentioned to my wife the possibility of applying for the post, she reminded me of the historical associations of the parish, of which, at that time, I was totally unaware. I applied anyway, and to my great surprise, not only was I called for interview, but was subsequently offered the job. We were expecting our second daughter at the time of the move, so life wasn't all that easy. We were offered accommodation in the no-longer-used house of the headmaster of the local village school – the head choosing instead, and probably quite sensibly, to live in the next village. The house, situated in the centre of the village was a cold, stone building with two bedrooms, study, sitting room, kitchen and a coal house converted into a downstairs bathroom and toilet, and was adjacent to the churchyard – a mere one minute's walk from the church.

Outisde our house in Bladon with two of our three children – Rebecca, myself, Jill, and Sarah.

We moved from Redditch to Bladon in the September of 1964, little realising what lay ahead. I can remember walking through the churchyard a couple of days after we had moved in, and meeting up with one of the parish's elderly parishioners – a Miss Savill, one of three spinster sisters. I still remember the gist of the conversation. She, after the usual pleasantries, pointed to a grassy grave space in the lee of the church tower, and asked, "Do you know who is going to be buried there?" I had learnt my priestly skills by then, or at least some of them. One didn't say 'yes', for fear of one's subsequent ignorance being found out. Neither did one reply 'No' for fear of being thought ignorant. "Do tell me" I replied, believing her to be about to tell me it would be a relative of hers, or some other influential parishioner, which in a way, it was. "Winston Churchill" she replied. I had no answer! I made my excuses, and made off, to report this strange conversation to my wife. She immediately explained that Sir Winston Churchill was of the Marlborough family, and Bladon was the Estate church of Blenheim Palace – a fact of which I had been totally unaware when I had applied for the job. But that was just the start. I thought no more about the conversation until that December. I went about my parochial duties, getting to know my parishioners, taking the services, interviewing couples requiring baptism for their children, organising a Sunday School, Church Choir and Youth Group, and planning a Confirmation preparation course.

Taken by surprise

In January 1965, it happened. The papers were full of it, it was on the radio and the television, and still I was hardly aware of how it was about to change my life. The reports came in that Sir Winston Churchill had fallen ill, very ill. It was therefore natural for me, at the Sunday service on the 17th of January, to remember Sir Winston and his family in the Sunday intercessions. Little did I expect to be front-page news in the Oxford Mail and the Daily Telegraph the following day. The Oxford Mail reported, "The Revd. John Fearn, Curate at Woodstock, said: "Let us pray for all who are sick, and especially at this time for Winston Spencer Churchill, that he may be spared discomfort, suffering and pain in these anxious days." The Daily Telegraph was more accurate; "At Bladon Church, Oxfordshire, where Sir Winston worshipped as a boy, the curate at the morning service, the Rev. John Fearn asked the congregation to pray specially for Sir Winston to be "spared discomfort, suffering and pain". A week later, he was dead.

I remember so well the morning that he died. It was the following Sunday. As usual, I had, the night before, compiled appropriate intercessions for the following day, and prepared my sermon. It was about 7.30 a.m., and I was in the bathroom with the radio on. I always liked to keep my Sunday prayers 'up to date', so I listened to the radio, in anticipation of any dramatic news item – a world disaster, or assassination. And then the announcement came.. Sir Winston Churchill had died during the night. I had no sooner taken this in, when the telephone rang. It was my Rector, making sure I was aware of the news, so that he and I could make appropriate changes to the tenor of our morning Services. I quickly finished my ablutions, got dressed, and hurried to the study to re-vamp my intercessions and re-write my sermon.

I was innocent, I was naive and I was totally unprepared for what was to come. The events of the next twelve months would provide enough material for at least a dozen books; here I must concern myself with my ministry, both locally, and as it turned out, internationally. I had a 'parish' of about a thousand people, of which five hundred (approximately) were Methodists, centred on Bladon's other place of worship, the Wesleyan Chapel, and five hundred Anglicans, both nominal and practising. We had a congregation of between twenty-five and forty most Sundays, and sixty or so at the festivals. That basically didn't change much, even after the funeral, although we were called upon to play host to quite a few visitors on Sundays, some of whom were accommodating and pleased to join us for the services, and some of whom were just a nuisance, and insisted on coming into the church, even during the services, to look around and to buy postcards. But I get ahead of myself. I must deal first with the preparations for the Committal Service, and the day of the Burial, and how it affected the church, the parish and me.

After lunch on the day that Sir Winston died, the Rector rang me, and explained that he had been in touch with Lady Churchill, and that the funeral had been arranged for the following Saturday in St. Paul's Cathedral in London, followed by the committal in Bladon Churchyard on the same afternoon. After the full panoply and ceremonial of the state funeral, there would be little left to do, according to the rites and Prayer Book of the Church of England, at the service of committal.

However, John James the then Rector graciously offered to share these simple last rites with me, inviting me to officiate with the 'Sentences' as the cortege was led from the Lych-gate to the graveside, he then offering the commendatory prayers at the burial. It was therefore during the days before the funeral that any parishioner abroad in the churchyard after dark would have seen me in my cloak, walking from the lych-gate to the graveside, muttering the sentences. I was (or rather I have always tried to be) a perfectionist; I wanted to get it right on the day - the right number of sentences, said at the right speed as I walked, so that I ended up in the correct position at the graveside at the conclusion of the last sentence. I am pleased to add that all my rehearsals stood me in good stead – on the day, it all worked perfectly.

Village preparations

The days that followed were the centre of great activity. By now it was acknowledged that Bladon would be the focus of international interest. The Highways department came along and painted double yellow 'no parking' lines throughout the village, on both sides of the road. Then the road-surfacing department came along and scraped off the road surface to a depth of about three inches and re-laid some brand new tarmac. Then the Highways department came back, and *again* painted double yellow 'no parking' lines right through the village for the second time. Outside our house on the opposite side of the road was the 'White House' Public House – named, no doubt after the Marlborough family's connection with the United States. Outside the pub was the village telephone. One morning early, workmen arrived with jack-hammers (pneumatic drills to you and me). By the end of the day, there was a row of six red telephone boxes – presumably, for the use of the press. This was in the days before mobile phones.

Lady Churchill had made the specific request that on the day of the funeral, there should be no visible presence of journalists, reporters or photographers in the village of Bladon. There were the days when the press, for the most part, respected such a request. So journalists had arranged with parishioners whose homes overlooked the route – perhaps, in some cases, for pecuniary advantage – to rent rooms, or at the least 'window' space on the day, so that they could subsequently write their accounts of the day from within the atmosphere of the village occasion.

Jill, my wife and I had been approached by two charming journalists from 'across the pond', Jane Armstrong of the Toronto Telegram and Gwen Morgan of the Chicago Tribune. They asked us if they too could be in our house 'on the day'. We readily agreed (but not, I hasten to add, for pecuniary advantage!) How naïve I was in those days! There was only one snag to all these arrangements. The police, fearing uncontrollable crowds, decided to impose a curfew on the village, from 8.00 a.m. on the day of the funeral until after the family and their party had left the churchyard following the committal. This meant that all journalists and reporters either had to be up very early, or be 'in situ' overnight, and this is exactly what our two lady journalists decided. They slept, uncomfortably I fear, on the couch and armchair in our sitting room.

The day itself

The next day was to be the most memorable of my entire ministry. John James the Rector had directed that I should take the 8.00 a.m. Holy Communion Service in Woodstock church that morning, so at about 7.40 a.m. I set off in my trusty Morris Minor Traveller for the parish church about three miles away. Nobody had told me that a cordon was being placed around the whole village of Bladon at 8.00 a.m. that morning. I took the service, arriving back in Bladon at about 8.55 a.m. to be met by a policeman in the middle of the road on the outskirts of Bladon, forbidding me access. I tried to explain that I lived in Bladon. He asked whether I had known about the cordon. I replied that I hadn't. He was obviously suspicious. He asked me for identification. I had none – I was in my cassock, with no wallet, no identifying documents. He was adamant. So was I. In the end I resorted to the persuasive argument: "If you don't let me through, there'll *be* no funeral!" Eventually he let me pass.

I arrived home to find everyone up, dressed, and watching the television over breakfast. I need to explain that our house was set some way back from the churchyard, at the northernmost end. The only view of the church and the site of Sir Winston Churchill's grave was through a tiny lancet window, half-way up the narrow staircase.

Our two lady journalists asked Jill if, during the actual service of committal, they could watch for a fleeting second or two, so that they could write, with veracity, "we looked, we saw, we were there". They insisted that my wife should have the lion's share of the viewing occasion. It was very strange watching the ceremonial of the procession from the lying in State at the Palace of Westminster, to St. Paul's Cathedral, knowing that it was all going to end up at Bladon. Together we watched the service in the cathedral, and the Churchill family as they emerged. Then followed the procession of the cortege down to the River Thames. Then the trip across the river. The great cranes alongside the wharves dipping in a final mark of respect. Then the short journey to Waterloo station and the placing of the coffin aboard the train, to be drawn by the great steam locomotive, 'Winston Churchill'. As the train pulled slowly out of the station, I remember saying to my wife and the others in the room; "Well, I must go now and put on my cassock, and go up to the church, to wait for the cortege." It was unreal. But it happened.

I could write a book (and probably will) of the many, many events which occurred following that memorable day – the 'Churchill Years' - but those memories are not for now. They belong in an account of their own. This story is concerned mainly with my life in the ministry, and the events which moulded it and which influenced the changes in my attitude to ministry, liturgy, ecumenism, authority, the episcopacy and personal faith from the days of becoming a naive, young, impressionable and headstrong curate, to a wiser, more mature but somewhat disillusioned priest in retirement.

A view of visitors at Sir Winston Churchill's grave – taken from the church tower.

The memorial tablet over the grave of Sir Winston and Lady Clementine Churchill.

The Churchill family graves in the lee of the north side of the church tower.

The aftermath

So what effect did this momentous event have on my faith, my outlook as a priest in the church of the 1960's, and in my relationship with my immediate superior, and later, with my bishop? The days, weeks, months following the day of the funeral were on occasions quite stressful. To be besieged, every day, by hundreds, by thousands of those making pilgrimage, paying their respects, and later the tourists and sightseers had a marked effect on the amount of time I could give to my pastoral work in the village. And yet I saw it all for what it was – a golden opportunity to perform pastoral work on a much wider canvas. A ministry to visitors, as well as to my resident parishioners. Many, many times I was approached by those visiting the grave and churchyard with the plea, "Are you the parish priest? Can you spare me a moment?" Often, it was just to ask for details about the Churchill family, the other graves, and where they could buy postcards. But on several occasions, I found myself in the presence of anxious and worried souls who were looking for counselling, advice, and a listening ear. Many were the times I was late for lunch because I had been sitting in the back pew of the church, quietly listening to the out-pourings of some troubled soul.

In addition, I also found myself as a sort of unofficial "guardian" of the Churchill graves. Two examples are firmly embedded in my mind in this respect. On one occasion, I was walking through the churchyard on some errand or other; the churchyard path was about four or five wide in visitors, and, ever observant as I passed the grave, I noticed an American matron (I got used to spotting them after a while) – taking something out of her handbag. Whether it was curiosity or nosiness I do not know, but I stopped, and watched. In her hand she was holding a small hammer, about nine inches long. I tapped her on the shoulder. "Pray what are you going to do with that, madam?" I enquired. Her reply bowled me over. "I'm just going to chip a little bit off for the folks at home", she replied. "I've got a bit of Blenheim, and a bit of Stratford-upon-Avon, so I thought a little bit of 'Churchill' would complete the set". I cautioned her about the error of her ways, and threatened to confiscate the hammer, and her handbag, if she so much as looked as if she was going to carry out her threat. She apologised and passed on her way.

Some unusual visitors

The second event happened very early one morning, just before sunrise. My wife woke me, explaining that she thought she could hear a noise in the churchyard. I hastily threw on some clothes and went to investigate. Again, I could hardly believe what I saw. A group of about five or six members of the Harlem Globetrotters Basketball team, standing on and around the grave, accompanied by an elegant and quite beautiful young girl in a diaphanous, almost see-through dress, having fashion photographs taken whilst she strutted and posed.

Politely, but in no uncertain terms I told them where to get off (literally!), and saw them off the premises, with a cautionary word about impropriety.

Another 'early morning' incident happened during one of the coldest periods of my time there. I was awoken by a knock at the door at about 4.00 a.m. It turned out to be a Polish free-lance photographer, asking permission to take a photograph in Bladon churchyard. When I reminded him that it was still dark – and freezing cold! – he explained that he wanted a photograph of the sun rising behind the church. Being something of an amateur photographer myself, I could appreciate his concept, and so I agreed. He had one further request; could he please have the lights on in church, so that the colours of the stained glass windows would mingle with the colours of the rising sun. I hastily threw on some clothes, and walked with him up to church. I unlocked the vestry, put on the lights and re-locked the vestry. It was still dark. I waited with him for a while, getting colder and colder in the process. Meanwhile, he was setting up his camera. I realised then that it would be some while before he had finished, and so taking a bold leap of faith, I gave him the vestry door keys, and asked him to put out the lights and lock the vestry again before leaving. "When you've finished," I said, "why not come down to the house for a spot of breakfast." I knew then that I would not be able to get back to sleep! This he did, and within a very short space of time we had made another good friend.

Difficulties at some Church services
On of the greatest problems in the parish was trying to hold Baptisms. Not that we had many in the small parish that we were, but I do remember that, even with a polite notice on the outside of the door stating "Please do not disturb, there is a Service in progress", we still had people trying to get in, and in so doing interrupting the service. What was more awkward was that, as in most Anglican churches, the font was sited near the south door, and the service was continually interrupted by visitors rattling the doorknob and latch before reading the notice. Visitors from all walks of life, of all nationalities, races and creeds came to pay their respects at Bladon. Some were respectful of the church, the grave and the churchyard, others much less so. They came into church eating, and occasionally smoking. Sometimes with their pets. I well remember the afternoon when I happened to be just inside the church door, when in walked a woman with a dog on a lead. I politely reminded her that we did not really permit dogs in church, unless they were guide dogs for the blind. At this, she picked it up, and said, "Alright, I'll carry it then". She was obviously deciding to be awkward and controversial. So I dug my toes in. "NO dogs in church, please," I said, emphatically, "whether walking, or on a lead." To which she replied, "This isn't a dog, it's a bitch!" I was nearly lost for words, but not quite. "Outside, please, " I replied, "NOW!"

At this time, I was also waging a literary war against the inaccuracies in the National press. The most blatant piece of misrepresentation came from the Daily Mail, who reported, at the beginning of February that, "More than £300 had been dropped into a collection box *nailed on the side of the church since Saturday.*" I wrote to the editor in the strongest possible terms to point out that the notice on the porch door, inviting passers by to contribute to the upkeep of the church had been in position long before I had ever been curate and that the wording of his article made the church out to be a money-grubbing organisation. I received an even more astounding reply. "I am extremely sorry to note that you misread our report which was, perhaps, quite unintentionally ambiguous, What we intended to convey, of course, was that £300 had been put into the collection box *'since Saturday'*, and not that the box had been nailed to the Church 'since Saturday'." The editor then confounded his error even further by ending with these words. "Although I agree that the sentence might have been better constructed, I do not think that in the context there was any real confusion in meaning." No apology. No retraction. I replied with a curt note suggesting that he and all his editorial staff would benefit from a course and exam at 'O' level in English Language!

Another 'howler' concerned a picture of my verger's wife, on the Friday morning photographed blowing her nose (she had a bad cold that day) whilst standing outside the church lych-gate, watching the final rehearsal for the committal. The photograph bore the caption, "*Villagers weep as they watch the weighted coffin being lowered into the grave*". What was even more amusing was that Jean Hall was standing some eighty yards from the grave, facing in the wrong direction!

Another 'classic' error appeared in the London Evening Standard on the day of the funeral. The caption under the picture of the church declared, "The quiet country churchyard at Bladon... ...through the black misty woods ...Blenheim". The only snag was that it wasn't a photograph of Bladon Church; it was Westerham Church in Kent!

Growing in Ecumenical understanding

I became much more ecumenical over the next few months than I had ever been in my life, or during my years in training, or in my early ministry. This was partly due to the fact that I was meeting members of other denominations, and people of other religions on a regular basis. It was interesting, it was informative and it was educational, but it also brought its problems. On Good Friday afternoon, I was conducting a devotional 'Hour at the Cross'. I had held the same sort of service, with the same hymns, readings, and similar addresses for several years. A fortnight later, I was summoned to the Bishop's house, with the requirement that I bring with me the text of my Good Friday sermons. The Bishop then told me that he had had a letter of complaint from a 'visitor' at the Good Friday Service, who was accusing me of preaching anti-Semitism. When I asked what it was that I was supposed to have said, I was told that I had, in the course of my discourse, said the "the Jews had cried out, 'Crucify Him, 'Crucify Him'". I told the Bishop that I have never heard anything so stupid in all my life, and that if I couldn't preach the Cross, and Christ crucified as it is recorded in the scriptures, then it was a sad day for the Church of England. He agreed, but asked me to retract my anti-Semitic attack, and write a letter of apology to the complainant, which I refused to do. I don't think this endeared me much to my diocesan bishop, but I felt I just had to make a stand for what I fervently believed was right. At that point he dismissed me, telling me that he would deal with it himself. I never heard any more about it, but it was just one example of the difficulties I faced when confronting the 'establishment' and the authority of the church, and the 'power' of the episcopacy, who seemed to pay scant regard to the truth, and were prepared to ride roughshod over junior clergy without giving them much of a hearing. Worse was to come, although I didn't know it at the time!

The other memorable and highly amusing ecumenical memory centred round a particular Sunday morning. I was in the vestry, ready and waiting with the choir for the clock to strike. The vestry, unusually, was at the back of the church, so it was no distance from the vestry door to the main entrance to the church. I popped my head round the door to make sure all was well; my sidesmen and churchwardens were at that time otherwise engaged settling in some of the congregation, but I noticed a group of seemingly bewildered young men at the church door. I welcomed them, gave them books, and found them seats. I thought no more about it, although I did notice that they did not approach the altar at the time of communion. After the service, at the church door, I got into conversation with them. "Thank you for the service," their spokesman said. "We are German Roman Catholics, and that is why we did not receive the sacrament", he explained. "But", he continued, "when we get back to Germany we are going to have strong words with our priest. He has always taught us that the Church of England is anathema, completely in error, with a liturgy totally different from the Catholic Mass. We were fascinated by your Eucharist service," he went on, "which in all respects was exactly the same as ours at home". We felt very comfortable in church here this morning. Thank you!"

This was a time of 'split' ministry, part of my time being spent on parochial duties, both in Bladon and in Woodstock, with Deanery Synods and clergy meetings and the occasional Diocesan Conference, and the other part being taken up with the 'Churchill' side of my ministry. This involved not only the administrative duties of an enormous daily post-bag – letters of enquiry, requesting register searches to establish English links with Bladon from Americans, and the requests for the whereabouts of lost property, and some 'silly mail' as well – poetry, complaints and suchlike. It was not only of local origin – it came from all over the world. In addition there was the ordering and re-stocking of the large number of postcards sold each day to visitors, and counting, bagging and banking the hundred-weights of loose change that accumulated during the course of each day. On top of this were the pastoral responsibilities of meeting and talking to the folk who passed daily through the church and churchyard, and counselling those who needed a sympathetic ear. It was an international task; at times I reflected on John Wesley's concept, that "The world was my parish". Visitors who were in trouble or distress, unable to voice their problems to their own priest or minister, found it easier to seek my advice and help; as I've mentioned, many an hour was spent at the back of church in quiet counselling sessions.

THE ILLUSTRATED LONDON NEWS—JULY 17, 1965

PERSONALITIES OF THE WEEK

Accompanying Lady Spencer-Churchill and Mary and Christopher Soames to Sir Winston's grave in Bladon Churchyard. (Copyright sought but untraceable).

Further Problems in the Parish

It was during the Christmas of 1965 that my life began to go pear-shaped. My Rector, responsible for the whole ecclesiastical parish of Bladon and Woodstock, tended to keep himself at Woodstock for most of the time, and left me to look after Bladon. Woodstock had a traditional pattern of Services – an 8.00 a.m. service of Holy Communion, an 11.00 a.m. Matins or Sung Eucharist, and Evensong at 6.30 p.m. At Woodstock he had the assistance of several Lay readers. Bladon on the other hand had a Parish Communion service at 9.15 a.m., and Evensong at 6.30 p.m. About once a month, so as to remind Bladon that they did in fact have a Rector, we used to 'exchange altars' – I would travel to Woodstock for the early Communion at 8 a.m., and John James would come over to Bladon to take the 9.15 a.m. service. For the rest of the time, he would concern himself with matters in Woodstock – a busy market town that included the Blenheim estate – home of the Duke of Marlborough. As I understood it, John James quite regularly enjoyed the hospitality of the Marlborough family, a privilege that I was never invited to share in, but this was of no consequence to me whatsoever. After the funeral of Sir Winston Churchill, I was left responsible for all the extra administrative and pastoral duties that followed, unless the church and grave was being visited by someone of importance, when the Rector advised me that he would be making himself responsible for that particular visit. I do however recall one delightful occasion during the summer when I was telephoned by Mary Soames, Sir Winston Churchill's daughter. Would it be convenient to meet her, her mother and Christopher Soames at the churchyard on a certain day the following week? Being aware of the protocol, I suggested that she should telephone John James, as I knew he would far rather be present, it being a family visit. To this suggestion, Mary Soames replied that she had already telephoned the Rectory, but was given to understand that the Rector was on holiday, and could I be there instead? I was delighted, but John James wasn't so enamoured when I broke the news to him on his return!

When it came to the Christmas Services in 1965, the understanding was that we would 'exchange altars' for the early morning services; I would take the 8.00 a.m. early morning service at Woodstock, and the Rector would take the extra 8.00 a.m. service at Bladon. I duly took myself over to Woodstock in good time to celebrate the Holy Communion, and in due course, returned to find several Bladon parishioners in some distress, wondering why I had not turned up at St. Martin's church, to take their Christmas Day early morning Communion. I was at a loss as to how to answer, except to explain that it was a 'swap' arrangement, and that the Rector should have turned up to take the service. I telephoned him, only to be answered by his wife, to be informed that he was 'unwell', this being the reason why he had not come over to Bladon. No messages, though, and no apology to the Bladon parishioners. Not only were my parishioners distressed, so too was I. To miss *any* service was unthinkable in my eyes – to miss the main early morning Christmas Day communion service was inexcusable, especially as no apology was forthcoming, either then, or later. And so it was that I later discovered the nature of the Rector's early Christmas morning 'malaise'. He had been at Blenheim Palace the previous evening, following the Midnight Mass, and, if the rumours that circulated the following week are to be believed, he was still 'in his cups' the following morning. I was horrified. When next I had the opportunity, I expressed my dismay not only at the circumstances of the missed service, but also at the lack of an appropriate apology. For this I was censured. Although the incident has slipped into the 'almost forgotten' past, I well remember that the end result was that both of us were required individually to state our respective cases, on separate visits, to the Diocesan Bishop. I do remember, at my interview, emphasising the lack of apology, for which situation I had the support of my parishioners, including the churchwardens and PCC treasurer; but it was all to no avail. At one stage during the Episcopal interview, the Bishop asked me how I would have dealt with the matter, to which I replied, "I would have had both of us here, *together*, in front of you my Lord, to get to the truth of the matter." The reply amazed and astounded me. "Your Rector *refuses* to come here to a meeting *with* you!" At this point I became so frustrated with the hierarchy's total lack of authority, and my inability to obtain justice and reason, I fear I went a bit too far. "In that case", I replied, "I might just as well resign my orders and make my living driving a taxi or a 'bus." From that time onwards, the Rector and I hardly spoke again; I received instructions for my duties via the telephone, with messages passed via his wife; I was still obliged to travel to the Rectory in Woodstock every Monday morning for a staff meeting, only to be met each time at the door by the Rector's wife who told me that he didn't wish to see me, nor did he have anything to say.

Preparing to move on
Despite this antagonistic attitude, I was still held in high regard by the parishioners of Bladon, who had supported me wholeheartedly throughout the whole, sordid business. Their solidarity and support was visibly demonstrated by the generosity of their gifts and good wishes at my leaving party some ten months later. For the final eight months of my ministry in Bladon, I was in constant touch with the Bishop, who went to great lengths I believe, to find me an appropriate and worthwhile move. On the 14th September, after a few inappropriate parishes had been suggested to me, I went to look at the parishes of Ruscombe and Twyford in Berkshire, a couple of parishes held in plurality, still within the diocese of Oxford. I remember going over with my wife on a 'pre-official' visit, to look the parishes over - to have a private 'snoop'. My wife and I went first to Twyford, an expanding dormitory community for London commuters with a fairly dark and gloomy mid-nineteenth century flint-faced church. One of the ladies of the parish was inside, polishing pews. Despite the fact that I was in 'mufti', I'm sure she 'spotted' me as a potential candidate for the job – the living being vacant at the time. I do remember saying to my wife, as we drove up to the other church, "I do hope it is not red-brick; I don't think I would care particularly to worship in a red brick church, after the atmosphere at

Bladon!" At that precise moment, we came around the corner, and there was Ruscombe Church – in all its red-brick glory!! But I did come to love that church; it was twelfth century brick, and it was an absolute gem of a building – it simply oozed the faith of the faithful of centuries. At that stage, I needed time to think – but, as the scriptures say '...it seemed good to the Holy Spirit and to me...". It must have done, because the interview that followed was a success - although one of the interviewers apparently was later reported to have commented, "He's a *bit young*, isn't he; I was hoping for someone a little more mature...." Two months later we moved to Twyford.

The Farewell parish Party and presentation at Bladon prior to leaving for Twyford.

Chapter 12

BERKSHIRE – RUSCOMBE & TWYFORD
1967 – 1985

Although we had moved to the 'living' of the parishes of Ruscombe and Twyford, we found ourselves housed in an enormous, modern, four-bedroomed Vicarage at Ruscombe, the smaller of the two communities, just over the road from the church. Twyford 'village' – it was more like a small, dormitory town - and church - were approximately seven-tenths of a mile away. It was a magnificent geographical centre for shops and other amenities; Henley-on-Thames was to the immediate north of us, Maidenhead about seven miles to the east; Wokingham to the south, and Reading about eight miles due west. Windsor, with its excellent theatre was also within easy range, and by car along the M4, London was also within fairly easy reach.

The 19th Century flint Church of St. Mary the Virgin, Twyford.

My new parish

Ecumenically it was an interesting situation; Twyford had a Congregational Chapel, and at the time of my arrival, a Roman Catholic congregation who attended Mass each Sunday in a temporary Nissen hut on the edge of the village. 'Village' was a misnomer – it was a community of some ten thousand people – a commuter community for both Reading and London – there being a first class train service to Paddington. Like Woodstock, Twyford Church started life as a 'Chapel of Ease' to the Parish church of Hurst, some four or five miles away, in the days when Twyford - 'the place of two fords' was little more than a hamlet. But with the industrial revolution came the railways, and with the railway came Twyford Station. It is said that the architect of Twyford Church was ordered to design a church, 'whose tower could be seen by passengers passing through the village on the railway'. Twice enlarged to accommodate the growing congregation, the church had little to commend it – it was a typical, dark, gaunt Victorian monstrosity with narrow lancet windows, an enormous nave, and a chancel so long, that on the first occasion that I celebrated Holy Communion at the High altar, with (as it was in those days) my back to the congregation, I felt as if I was on another planet. Even when I turned around, I could hardly see the more recalcitrant members of the congregation who were determined to sit in the furthest possible pew, right at the west end of the church.

By this time, we had three small children, all under five years of age. One of my first tasks, therefore, at the Vicarage was to erect wire netting around the perimeter of the extensive garden, to prevent their escape. Whilst engaged on this task, I was spotted by a parishioner; it wasn't long before the story got around that the 'new' vicar was obviously into 'keeping hens'!

As you can imagine, I was thrilled at the prospect of my own living, my own parishes, all my own responsibility, although the prospect was not a little daunting. Imagine my disappointment then when, just prior to my Service of Licensing, the Bishop took me on one side in the vestry and explained to me that, for legal and technical reasons, and although I would be called 'Vicar' by all my parishioners, I was, by ecclesiastical law, being licensed as 'a perpetual curate'. I could hardly believe my ears! What a time to tell me! This actually meant that I would not hold the living 'in perpetuity' nor did I have what, in those days, was termed 'the Parson's freehold'. However, I put a brave face on it, and processed into church to meet my new parishioners. Being new to the game, I had agreed to the service being prepared in advance; in hindsight, I would have rather have had some input into its construction. It was a fairly traditional affair, with hymns I personally would not have chosen.

Having played second fiddle to a Vicar and later to a Rector for some years, it was strange now to be addressed as 'Vicar'; indeed, initially I had to stop myself turning round on more than one occasion, to see where 'he' was! I don't remember much about those early months in the parish, probably because I was so busy getting to know everybody and learning how the parish 'ticked'. They were a grand group of people in the church fellowship, both contemporary in age and older, and I think that most of them took to me as easily as I took to them.

The delightful red-brick and flint Church of St. James the Great, Ruscombe

Churchmanship - High, or Low?

My predecessor in the parishes it seemed had been an 'everything to all men' sort of priest; at Twyford he had followed a more Anglo-catholic tradition, and he told me that I was expected to wear a lace cotta, stole and biretta when celebrating at Twyford, and a surplice, hood and scarf at Ruscombe. Mercifully, I was not expected to celebrate from the 'North end'. I made it quite clear to both parishes right from the beginning that I was 'me', and that I did not believe in partisanship; services in both churches would be identical, I would wear vestments at both churches, and choir robes for non-eucharistic services. Nobody minded a bit – in fact I have a feeling they were quite relieved!

This decision seemed to have had a beneficial effect on churchgoing right from the start. No longer did parishioners feel that they had to gravitate towards one particular 'brand' of churchmanship. Apart from the bigoted few who were not happy with my middle-of-the-road approach to catholic-evangelicalism, or was it evangelical-catholicism? – and who left to join other churches more suited to their religious practices - the majority of church members now had a wide ranging choice of services to attend to fit in with their Sunday routines. For me it was a fairly tight Sunday service schedule. I started with an 8.00 a.m. said Service of Holy Communion at Twyford, then back to the vicarage for a quick coffee before taking a 9.00 a.m. (said) service of Holy Communion at Ruscombe, then another quick, 'ready-to-drink' coffee from the Vicarage hall table, and straight on down to a 10.00 a.m. (fully choral) Sung Eucharist at Twyford. This was followed immediately by a poorly attended fully choral Matins at 11.15 a.m. Two Sundays out of four I had Holy Baptisms in the afternoon, culminating with Evensong at one or other of the churches at 6.30 p.m.

I do remember that after about three or four weeks of this hectic routine, I actually fell asleep over my Sunday roast! Obviously things had to change. It was not the multiplicity of services that was particularly bothering me, but rather the fact that I didn't have time to talk to anyone after the services – and this to my mind was a crucial, pastoral opportunity. So we moved the 10.00 a.m. service forward to 10.30 a.m., and rid ourselves of the anachronistic fully choral Matins, which had a maximum attendance of about ten, excluding the choir, who had already sung a fully choral Eucharist only minutes before. Of course there was dissent, the strongest voices raised being those on the P.C.C. who rarely if ever attended Matins! Another change that took place around this time was the rationalisation of the multiplicity of Communion Services. I argued that the joint parish - as I though of it - although there were some die-hards who were adamant that there still existed two distinct parishes, needed only one said Communion Service, and one choral Eucharist each Sunday. A simple survey of attendance numbers over a couple of years, with figures gleaned from the service registers, illustrated that the 8.00 a.m. service was the least well attended of all services, and that most of those who were eight o'clock adherents drove there by car. In point of fact, they could just as easily drive to Ruscombe for the nine o'clock Communion.

But tradition dies hard in the established Church of England; the secretary of my P.C.C. set up a petition for the retention of the early morning service; the Bishop was consulted, he agreed with the wisdom of my case for the re-alignment of services, and the dear PCC secretary, along with one or two others, left us and joined the congregation of a neighbouring church.

It was that same Bishop, whom I had met in the ante-room of the Crematorium Chapel some months before during the initial days of this new ministry. He gave me some very good advice. "In the eyes of your parishioners", he said, "for the first twelve months, you can do nothing wrong. They are getting used to you, and you are getting used to them." But, he added, "During the second year, they expect you to remember them all by name, and are most displeased if you don't. By your third year, you will begin to feel that you cannot do anything right!" My 'third year' had already arrived!

The fracas subsided, and life settled into a more rational, sensible pattern. As a result of the changes, more people that ever started attending morning services; although in the eyes of my brother clergy, it was almost sacrilegious to do away with an established, 8.00 a.m. Communion service, but it made sense to me. The 8.00 a.m. service was a 'left over' from the previous patterns of worship of yester-year when, in ninety-nine out of a hundred Anglican churches, the eight o'clock Communion was for the devout, eleven o'clock Matins was for the upper classes whilst the servants prepared lunch, and a six o'clock Evensong was for the particularly devout, and the servants. Indeed, there is a charming church in Worthen in north Shropshire which I came across later in my ministry, where the 'comfortable' pews were around the walls of the church, and there were back-less 'benches' for the servants down the middle of the nave.

Developing pastoral work in the Parish

The nine o'clock morning Communion service at Ruscombe became a very popular time for worship. It gave busy commuters a bit of a lie in on a Sunday morning, and yet ended in time for them to get away to visit relatives for Sunday lunch. This was important in the community in which I now found myself. It was an expanding, commuter 'town-ship' mostly comprising young families with one, two or three children. Keeping pace with their details was difficult – this was in the days before computerised parish records. They came into the parish, and I discovered this when I was called upon to arrange the baptism of their newly born infants. Then they had a second child, and looked for a slightly bigger house. This way, they spent a lot of energy moving around the parish; some moved out, and some moved in, and some just moved around!

The next development was self-creating – the need for a Sunday School. There were four schools in the immediate area – a Church controlled Infant School, a State Junior School, a State controlled Primary school, and a Church of England Secondary School. Hundreds, thousands of children in the parish. We ended up with a four-Department Sunday School to cater for both the geographical and age needs of the children. Twenty teachers, fifteen helpers, weekly preparation classes, and a monthly Family Service which almost filled Twyford church to its 350 seat capacity. As the Sunday School grew, so we needed more accommodation – we ended up with the Sunday School in three venues; the older children in Ruscombe Church, and two primary sections, one in each of the two local Primary schools, which served the parish well, because the buildings were already familiar to all the local children who attended.

One of Twyford's older residents regaled me with a delightful account of the church in earlier days. Once a year as a Sunday school outing, all the children of the Sunday School processed behind the church processional cross from the church at Twyford right through the village to the quite extensive grounds of Ruscombe Vicarage for their annual Sunday school treat! After races on the vicarage lawn, they were treated to a tea of sandwiches, cakes, jelly and orange squash. By the time I had arrived and the Sunday school had been re-established, the children expected a somewhat more sophisticated annual treat. One in particular comes to mind; three coach loads of children, parents and teachers spending a day at Butlins' holiday camp at Littlehampton in Sussex. I was press-ganged into riding with some of the children on a precipitous 'Big Dipper' roller-coaster which I undertook with a brave face. My other memory was the sad occasion when two of our more deprived boys, having looked forward to the outing for many weeks, were immediately taken round the shops by their mother on arrival in Littlehampton, only to catch up with the coach again just before we again left for home.

The lasting impression they left behind was the disastrous effect of the journey home, when they brought back up the hamburgers to which they had been treated just prior to their departure. Luckily, being forewarned by several experienced mothers, we had had the foresight to take with us on the coach a pile of newspapers, buckets and mops- but the occasion still sticks in my mind as a somewhat malodorous return trip!

Worship

One of the next changes I introduced was a sermon at the nine o'clock said morning Communion service. As in the days of the 'old 8 o'clock', which many had attended as a 'be all and end all' act of Sunday devotion, it occurred to me that these early morning parishioners were regularly receiving the sacrament, but never the 'Word'. Since I had been ordained to 'administer both the Word and the Sacraments', this was what I now intended to do. So I started with a short, tern-minute homily. Some of the congregation complained, but the majority saw the sense of my argument, and the congregation increased yet again. One dear lady, a former churchwarden, sitting at the back, used regularly to look pointedly, at her watch. To my knowledge she never actually shook it, to see if it was still working! One day, I could resist the temptation no longer. I was at the end of my sermon. I looked straight at her, pausing until I had her attention. "I've nearly finished!" I said. She took it in good part, and never looked at her watch so obviously ever again.

Worship in both our churches had until then had been fairly formal occasions, involving only 'regular' churchgoers. I felt that a further change was due. We needed to be a 'missionary' church, practising 'outreach' to those beyond the regular church congregation. We needed to involve *families* on a regular basis. Having discussed the implications with the P.C.C., I devised a less formal 'Family' Communion service, to be held in Twyford Church on the first-Sunday-of-every-month. It was coming up to Mothering Sunday, and that was the date I settled on for its introduction. Invitations were sent out to every family that had had a child baptised in the previous twelve months, to every family with children in our Sunday School, to all members of the Mother's Union, the Youth Group and everyone on the Church Electoral Roll, along with anyone else who came to mind. Within the strict rules of the Prayer Book, I 'relaxed' the service, making judicious excisions, and employing modern language for the scriptures and intercessions. Were it to happen today, I would have gone much, much further, but I had in the back of my mind the 'charge' at my ordination, "...to obey my Ordinary (bishop) and other chief Ministers of the Church ...*and to use such services.....*" By now, and with the memories of the twentieth century Church Light Music group still ringing in my ears from my college days, I was aware of several 'modern' hymns with 'catchy' tunes – which I also included in the service. Came the day – I remember processing into church, and seeing a vast crowd, filling the church. There was only one snag – I had contracted laryngitis! How was I ever going to make myself heard from the nave altar, never mind the pulpit? These were the days before we had installed our 'public address' loudspeaker system; that was to come much later. However, it was an absolutely fantastic occasion, noisy – but *so* satisfying. There were children of all ages, from babes in arms to teenagers; there were young parents, grandparents and a few octogenarians. From push-chairs to bath-chairs, almost! It had happened. It had worked. Sadly, some of the younger families with noisy babies were a bit embarrassed, but I quickly found a solution to put them at their ease. "Take them for a walk around the church," I advised; "show them the stained glass windows. A child on the move is a happy child" I suggested. It worked. Parents got over their initial embarrassment, and the service proceeded to its conclusion. I was delighted. I had shouted myself hoarse from the pulpit, and by the end I was speechless, literally. But it didn't matter. It had been a success. Praise the Lord!

Because legally, Ruscombe and Twyford were two parishes held 'in plurality', they were independent of each other. For the parishioners, this hardly mattered at all. Those Ruscombe people who fancied a Sung Eucharist worshipped at Twyford, and those who preferred an earlier 'said' service came up to Ruscombe; no-one kept rigidly to their parish boundaries. There were, however, one or two Twyford young people who were keen on getting married in the much more convenient, photogenic church at Ruscombe. It only seated seventy or so, the average size of a wedding congregation, so the whole feeling was much more intimate and friendly – a 'full' church. Twyford by comparison was a great barn of a building, in which wedding congregations rattled around.

These were the days when the Church of England was beset by rather silly rules and regulations [was it ever not?], couples having to be married in the parish church of one of the couple, was one such rule. It seemed it was all to do with the popularity of photogenic churches, and stemmed from the time when a parson's fees were augmented by the payments (fees) due to him for marriages. Any relaxing of the rules would have made multi-millionaires of incumbents of 'photogenic' churches in idyllic rural settings, and the incumbents of gothic 'monstrosities' built during the industrial revolution would have ended up penniless, despite their much larger populations. I tried to observe these niceties, but rules, I was told, were made to be broken, and one system very prevalent at the time, especially in my 'patch', was the leaving of a suitcase in the home of a relative for three weeks in an appropriate parish, and by so doing, claiming a 'residential' qualification for the reading of 'Banns'.

Parish administration

It may have been satisfactory for the parishioners, but it made my life difficult. Although each Parochial Church Council had its own need to discuss domestic church matters such as maintenance, drains and expenditure at meetings roughly once every two months, this was also a time of forthcoming changes in the Church at large, all of which were required to be discussed in P.C.C. Marriage discipline was one, I remember; Christian Initiation (Baptism and Confirmation) another and the modernisation of worship a third. P.C.C. members had to discuss them only once; I had to go through the whole exercise twice, every time. I explained the foolishness of this system to my churchwardens and P.C.C.'s, and got them to agree to a more sensible arrangement. From then on, short 'business' meetings were held to discuss matters pertinent to each individual church building, and 'joint' meetings to discuss these wider issues. This not only saved me time and energy, but it had a far wider-reaching goal – it ensured that members of P.C.C.'s and congregations that normally never met one another, did just that. They shared experiences and opinions, and got to know one other. This was to prove an excellent foundation for the next stage of the plan to bring them closer together, the creation of a 'United Benefice'.

One of the on-going concerns in such a large parish was one of finance. With the experience of the Christian Stewardship programme in my former parish [although the Redditch experience was more 'funding' than 'stewardship'], we decided to hold a major stewardship initiative in our two parishes, initially employing a professional organiser to head up our local team. The programme consisted of an 'every-member-canvass', much on the lines of the commercial 'Wells' funding exercise which I had experienced previously. Each listed church member was individually visited and invited to 'pledge' a realistic regular amount for the work of the Church in the parish, diocese and in the world. It worked.

One strange co-incidence occurred at this point in my ministry. I had been preparing for confirmation a young classics graduate named Janet Palmer, a regular member of the congregation, who was of an age and circumstance not to fit into any of the 'classes' I was running at that time. She was too old for the 'teenage' groups, and her time-table didn't allow her to participate in the adult group – so it became a one-to-one instruction. She had previously been doing library work, but had recently started working at the offices of the Church Commissioners in London, in the 'strategy' department. With the blessing of the Bishop and the consent of the P.C.C.'s, my two parishes eventually applied for 'United Benefice' status. When these plans, agreed by the Church Commissioners finally received the royal assent, we were sent a copy of the relevant Instrument.

It turned out by pure chance that this particular amalgamation was the first such 'Instrument' that Janet Palmer had been allowed to see through entirely on her own! The outcome of this legal move meant that we were no longer two independent parishes with separate P.C.C.'s, but one united benefice with two churches and a single P.C.C. This made for great fun when, at the next Annual

General Meeting, church folk were vying for the limited seats on the new P.C.C.! Competition was strong, and we applied the democratic rule of election by secret ballot.

With regard to the 'ordering of the Sunday services', this proved to be a nightmare, a liturgical minefield. At Communion Services, the 'Summary of the Law' was used extensively as an alternative to the Ten Commandments, despite the fact that it was illegal – forming as it did, part of the 'adopted' Prayer Book of 1928, which Prayer Book had been accepted by the church and authorised for use by the bishops, but which never received Parliamentary assent. The Collects for the Queen and Royal Family were often omitted, as certainly were the three 'exhortations', but an 'Agnus Dei' was often inserted, which had formed no part of the 1662 liturgy. The Church was beginning, illegally, to 'adapt' its worship to the needs of the people. The 'Experimental Liturgy' went several stages further but although the suggested changes seemed dramatic at that time, the one change that even the liturgical reformers weren't bold enough to suggest was the alteration of the accepted text from 'Thee' to 'You'. This wasn't to come about until much later. One bold move, however, came in 1982 with the publication of "Hymns for Today's Church" – a collection of traditional and contemporary hymns and better known choruses all re-written in the 'you' idiom. Sadly, it never caught on; churches were put off not only by their fear of upsetting 'traditional' members of their congregations, but also by the initial cost of introducing it throughout their churches. But by this time, I had found a simple solution; I had produced a loose-leaf hymn-book of some 100 hymns, collected from a diversity of sources for use alongside the traditional one.

Another 'avant-garde' action which I took during my ministry in Berkshire was the practice I introduced each Christmas of getting together a band of singers - drawn from the Border (Youth) club, its leaders, parents and parishioners, and touring around the parish 'singing carols for the joy of it'. One particular instance involved a visit to the local old folks' bungalows on the Orchard Estate in Twyford – independent bungalows for the retired which had a central, communal lounge where they gathered (as many as wanted to) for evening social activities. We called in, and sang our first carol. When it was finished, the old folks immediately reached for their purses and back pockets. What a pleasure it was to inform them that we were *not* collecting - neither for the church, nor for a charity, but were just singing for the joy of it. And so we asked them what carol they would next like us to sing. The residents could hardly believe their ears – but it taught us all a thing or two – not least, the youngsters in the group. We raised funds a-plenty during the course of the year for various missions and charities – I wanted to re-introduce the real spirit of Christmas, and sing without a collecting tin. It worked!

A review of life in Ruscombe and Twyford
I remember my eighteen years in Twyford and Ruscombe with gratitude and satisfaction. These were busy days, they were tiring, but they were absolutely

fascinating. There was never a dull moment and never two days the same. In addition to 'the trivial round, the common task...' – the daily round of services, parish visiting, trips to visit parishioners in hospital, school governors' and managers' meetings, and Baptism and Marriage interviews, there was always the unexpected. Like the day during an arms amnesty, when an ex-soldier turned up on my doorstep with a German Luger 9-mm pistol and the request, "Would I hand it in, please, anonymously to the police station", as he felt that it was a liability, hidden away in the top of his chest of drawers. The police subsequently wanted to know where it had come from, but I had given my word, so although fearing arrest and incarceration, I simply replied, "From World War II". Well, it was true! All was well.

We had a regular procession of tramps to the Vicarage door, often just asking for tea and sandwiches, which Jill and I were always happy to supply, and the recipients were, on the whole, grateful. All but one, that is, who remains memorable, but for perhaps the wrong reason. One day there was a knock at the door, and standing there on the porch step was one of the itinerant brotherhood, asking for money.

The first rule I had been taught was, *never* to give money – it would only be spent on alcohol or methylated spirits. I offered sandwiches and a cup of tea, which he reluctantly agreed would be an acceptable substitute. We had little food in the fridge – it was the end of the month. But we did have some cheese. So while I kept an eye on the doorstep, Jill made some sandwiches, and wrapped them up carefully in greaseproof paper and put them in a brown paper bag. Often, these 'gentlemen of the road' kept them for later. I gave him the sandwiches, with a mug of tea, which he immediately put on the ground. "What's in these?" he asked, as he undid the package. He opened one up. "Bloody cheese! No thank you" he said, scornfully, and handed them back to me, took his mug of tea and went off to sit in the church porch. "Suit yourself," I said, as he walked away, "I *thought* you said you were hungry?!"

A similar thing occurred when we were visited unusually, by an exceptionally stout and unkempt lady tramp, who also asked for money for food, this time ostensibly to feed her two starving children. I offered her a cup of tea and some sandwiches, but she declined. She then changed her story, and asked for money for a train fare to get her into Reading to the local Salvation Army hostel. I asked her where her children were, but she evaded the question. I became a little suspicious. When it became obvious to her that no money was forthcoming, she made to leave. I had discovered during our brief conversation that she was a Roman Catholic – she kept calling me 'Father'. When I explained that I was 'Church of England', she said, "You're all the same, you lot!" So I suggested she visited the Convent just the other side of the Bath Road – I knew the nuns well; they would at least have offered her facilities – a badly needed bath and a meal. We parted company on the front doorstep but my instinct told me that something was amiss. I let her leave, and then I followed her discreetly, to see which way she went. To my astonishment she got into an Austin A30 parked just around the corner, and drove off. I can only suppose she thought it was worth a shot! I immediately phoned the convent to warn them of her imminent arrival.

My most vivid memory…

My most vivid memory, certainly of my time in the parish, and probably of my whole ministry, was an occasion that is etched forever in my mind, and which is a condemnation of the Church as a whole, and its total lack of compassion and understanding. It concerns the church's pre-occupation with 'things', rather than 'people'. Shortly after my arrival in the parish, we had suffered a 'breaking and entering' at Ruscombe Church; a thief had broken into the church through a small, leaded north window behind the church – probably measuring not more than 16" by 18", some eight feet above the ground, and stolen the brass altar cross and candlesticks. I was outraged. As a result, the P.C.C. wanted to keep the church locked all day and night, except when in actual use. I strongly objected. I argued that even if everything in the church was stolen, I still wanted it kept open, at least during the day. It was a place of prayer, a refuge, and a sanctuary. So we ordered a cheap, replacement cross and candlesticks, I had them engraved on the reverse with the name of the Church (against considerable opposition – it was not the 'done thing, apparently because it 'detracted from their intrinsic value'!), and the church remained open during the hours of daylight.

One morning about 10.00 a.m., I went over to the church to collect a register and say my prayers. I noticed a car parked outside the church. Sitting, quietly sobbing in the back pew was a young mother. I went to my stall in the choir, knelt down and prayed for her. She didn't move, but just went on sitting there, quietly sobbing. Eventually, my prayers said, I approached her. "Do you want to be left alone" I enquired, "or would you like to talk?" She looked up. "Do you mind," she asked, "you don't even know me?" "Of course not," I replied. And so her story came out. She was in post-natal depression. She lived on the Isle of Wight. Things had been getting on top of her since the birth of her second child. One day (that day in fact) it had all overwhelmed her. She left her children with her mother-in-law, had got into the car, and had driven off to the ferry. She had no idea where she was going, but she had an idea of what she might do. The further away from Portsmouth she drove, the more desperate she became to find a church. One after another, she found them all locked. She drove on to another, and another, and then another. In her mind she was seriously considering committing suicide. She started looking for a convenient railway bridge.

She arrived at Ruscombe, where there were a railway line, a bridge and church. She played the dice game with herself. If the church was open, she would go in. If it was locked, like all the others, she decided that she would end it all, and throw herself in front of an oncoming train.

She found the door open. And that was where I found her. We talked – or rather, she talked and I listened. For hours. It all poured out of her. She became calmer. The tears dried up. "Do you think I've been silly?" she asked. "No, I don't," I replied, "but think of your husband, and your children, and how much they would have missed you. Why don't you come over to the Vicarage, and telephone your mother-in-law, and let her know you're alright. Then stop and have some lunch with us – there's only my wife at home – the children are all at school. And then, when you feel up to it, you can drive home to your children." She gave me a smile, and a brief word of thanks. I quickly told my wife the gist of the situation, and during lunch, we learnt a bit about her children, and her life on the island. We had once had a short holiday there, so conversation was easy, for we had places in common that we knew. After a cup of tea later in the afternoon she left for home, promising to 'phone me to let me know she had arrived safely, which she did. The aftermath? Every year for several years, we had a Christmas card from her and her family. All was well. And, I like to think it was because I insisted to the P.C.C. that the church remained open, even if everything was stolen, desecrated or vandalised. Little did I realise at the time how my remarks would come true, later in my ministry. But the text was in my mind, "Which shepherd does not leave his flock, and go after just one of his sheep in difficulties?"

On another occasion, a young man called at the Vicarage, also in some distress. His mind was in turmoil, but I gained the impression, as he talked, that he was in some way 'touched'. He was 'not quite right' – a sandwich short of a picnic. But he needed to talk, and so I listened. And listened. And listened. Eventually, he quietened down. He thanked me for listening and took his leave. I put the matter out of my head. And then, about three weeks later, I received a telephone call in the middle of a small dinner party. It was this chap again, claiming to be in a telephone box on Westminster Bridge. He said that if I didn't come down to London straight away to fetch him, he was going to throw himself in the river. I tried to reason with him; he had phoned me 'reverse charge' so we were on the 'phone for ages. But he was not to be turned away from his intentions. I tried to explain that over an hour's journey down to London was just not on the cards. He rang off. I telephone the police and told them the story. I had a very bad night that night, and avidly read the papers for the next few days. Thank goodness, no news of a river suicide. But I still couldn't be sure. And then it happened. I received another call. It was this chap again. Trying the same ploy. I suggested he visited one of the nearby London clergy for help, or the Salvation Army. He phoned on an irregular basis for quite a while, and then the calls stopped. I never heard from him again. But it all added to the stresses and strains of parish life in general, and my ministry in particular. But it was all in a day's work.

Christian Initiation
Following a series of conferences, seminars and clergy discussions on the subject of Christian Initiation (Baptism and Confirmation) and statutory discussions at P.C.C., I felt that the time was right for change in the way we introduced

newcomers into the church. I had never been happy about the custom of traditional Sunday afternoon Baptisms – they had always seemed to me to be 'hole-in-the-corner' occasions. I regularly asked myself the question, "*Why* do we do *what* we do? Is there any good reason for it, except tradition?" The Baptism service was referred to in the Prayer Book as 'The Service of *Public* Baptism' except where there were dire circumstances. When I had challenged the system as a curate in Redditch, I had always been told that the presence of some six to ten babies, accompanied by some sixty to a hundred parents, godparents, relatives and friends, constituted 'the Public'. It was with this assumption that I was profoundly unhappy. I wanted the *worshipping* congregation to be present to welcome new members into the family. At Twyford I was now in a position to instigate change, or at least introduce a little diplomatic alteration to the status quo. I was being asked to perform an average of six or so baptisms a month. I persuaded the P.C.C. to allow me to include the Baptism service into the main liturgies of the day – during the Holy Communion service at Twyford, and during Evensong at Ruscombe, on an average of once a month. Architecturally, Twyford church allowed four families to sit in the front blocks of pews and Ruscombe, with a simple central aisle, allowed for two.

I again re-vamped the service, so that the whole liturgy would take no more than an hour; this was becoming more and more possible with the advent of the official liturgical reforms based on the 1662 Book of Common Prayer. The Communion Service could end at the Gospel, when, after a short address, the Baptism could take place, and we could then pick up the service at The Peace. At Evensong, everything after the Third Collect was an accretion, so again, with a metrical Psalm and shortened canticles, the Baptism fitted neatly into the Service. What it meant, theologically was that families became part of the worshipping community, at least for one Sunday, and the congregation themselves began to take notice of, and responsibility for the newcomers into the Faith. Although I say it myself, and although it met with certain opposition from a few remaining 'die-hards', it worked. Of course some of the children were noisy, but we had the forethought to provide a whole library of appropriate children's books, and with a sympathetic "Why not take 'little one' for a walk around the church for a while", there was little enough distraction. The problem came, of course, on the occasions when the proud parents of a new baby came requesting a "private" Christening. Two such occasions come to mind from the days before the new system was introduced. I was visiting one such set of parents, and I explained that their entourage would all be seated on the left-hand side of the church, and the other family on the right. "What other family?" they asked indignantly. I explained the system, and that Baptism was a 'public' service at which their new offspring would be welcomed into the family of the church. Reluctantly, they concurred; I had given them little alternative! On the other occasion, I had agreed to an afternoon service, due to the numbers attending, but I made sure there would also be another family at the same service. When I was informed that there would be in excess of one hundred guests, not all of whom would be coming to the church service, I reminded the family that the other family would have as many 'priority' seats at the front of church as they were having. They too were not pleased. Nevertheless, I was invited to 'the knees up, to *wet the baby's head'* after the service. I explained that, being a Sunday afternoon, I had an evening service to take as well. "Oh, don't worry," I was told, "Come on later. The Party will go on well into the early hours; we've got the Lionel Blair Dancers around the swimming pool as entertainment, and drinks will be flowing freely all night". It was almost a case of nudge, nudge, wink, wink, if you know what I mean. I politely declined. It wasn't quite my idea of Christian initiation!

The Monthly Family Service
As far as Sunday services were concerned, the monthly Family Service was going from strength to strength. It quickly became a 'feature' of local church life, and as well as encouraging children into the church, provided a less formal vehicle for those who hadn't been to church for a while, to re-acquaint themselves with their parish church. It wasn't all plain sailing though; one strange phenomenon was that Sunday School children tended to come without their parents, and families who couldn't be persuaded to send their children to Sunday School, came without them to the Service. It hardly mattered, though, because we were filling the church month by month. At this point I devised what Baldrick in 'Blackadder' would have called a 'cunning plan'. I persuaded the P.C.C. to stick to their agreement to a 'first-Sunday-in-the-Month' plan, and then persuaded them that it would be liturgically wrong not to add into this programme of less formal Services the main festivals of the church's year. So, when Palm Sunday, Easter Day, Whitsunday, Christmas and Harvest didn't fall on a first Sunday in the month (Christmas Day was *very* unlikely!) we *still* had a Family Service. My reasoning was that those who came regularly and informally needed to be present at the church's main festivals. It worked like a charm !

One of the main features of these services was the introduction of visual aids, something memorable that the congregation would take away with them and on which to pin their thoughts. I think the most bizarre of all was the three-foot long grass snake that I borrowed from a local pet-shop; I had it wriggling around my hands in the pulpit for fifteen minutes whilst I preached on the story of Adam and Eve. It captivated the congregation, especially those sitting in the front pew, directly under the pulpit! I called him 'Fred' so as not to frighten the tinies, and most of the children came up after the service to stroke 'Fred" and ask questions. I hoped that some of them remembered the story of Adam and Eve as well.

On another occasion, on the Sunday after the parish Comfirmation, I used the Cliff Richard 'pop' song popular at that time and No: 1 in the charts – "Congratulations" to 'congratulate' those who had taken this further stage in their Christian life. That also worked. I found out afterwards that one family had gone out to Majorca for their holidays; the song was played incessantly over the swimming pool loudspeakers, and each time they heard it they remembered the post-Confirmation sermon!

On other occasions I used a boiling kettle on the pulpit edge – an illustration of 'zeal' – being boiling hot Christians. On another, at a Harvest Thanksgiving, I took into church an eight-foot Sunflower, and a sunflower seed – the marvel of God's creation. And on yet another occasion, I promised to show the congregation something that no-one in the world had ever seen before; I produced a melon and a sharp knife, slit open the melon, and extracted a seed on the pointed end of the knife – an illustration of God's continuing creative power. My innovative ideas used to cause some reaction from the traditionalists; I once placed a gallon can of Motor engine oil, a miner's core sample and a piece of coal on a window ledge in church, at a Harvest Thanksgiving, to illustrate the munificence of God's underground wealth and gifts. Some of the church ladies re-acted by saying that I ought only to have fruit, vegetables and flowers on display in church. I promptly reacted by designing a window with a packet of Cornflakes, a bottle of milk and a tin of sardines!

It was our custom, instead of distributing items from the harvest display to the elderly of the parish, which so often caused disagreements, to hold a 'Harvest Sale' at the entrance to the church drive on the Monday following Thanksgiving, in which I took a full part. The proceeds went to one of the 'food aid' charities. Having no idea of the cost of flowers, fruit and vegetables, I was relegated to the 'tins and packets' stall. I well remember one occasion when a pseudo-sophisticated non-church attending middle-aged female customer approached my stall, and after poking around among the tins for a while enquired: "Have you any sardines or pilchards in oil?" "No" I replied, "they've all gone. But I do have a tin here of pilchards in tomato sauce." "That's no good at all," she replied, "My cat doesn't like tomato sauce!" I was flabbergasted, and pleased in a way that I didn't have the required tin.

One Whitsunday, at Family Service, I was preaching on the first Pentecost, the 'birthday' of the church. Right at the end of the service, before we dispersed for refreshments, some of the mothers came up the aisle with an enormous birthday cake, with over a hundred candles lit, and we all sang a spontaneous "Happy Birthday" to the Church!

I must pay tribute to my organist at the time, Sybil Stephenson. Although not totally in tune with my advanced ideas for the forward thinking church, nor with my innovative services, choruses and hymns, she did go a long way towards following my lead. On one occasion there was a particularly noisy child in church, giving vent to its emotions just prior to the service. To my utter amazement, the organ voluntary faded out, and in its place came the unmistakable strains of 'Hush-a-bye baby, on the tree top...' from the organ loft. She didn't take kindly though, to some of my more innovative hymns. I had remembered, from my time on Blakang Mati Island off Singapore, the words [on film] of John Wesley, the great social and religious reformer. "Why should the devil have all the best tunes..?." Whether this actually originated with Wesley, or with William Booth has never really been established. However, I felt strongly that it contained an eternal truth. These were the days of the beginning of what has since developed into football fanaticism, the days of the regular, Saturday night programme, 'Match of the Day'. So I set about writing a hymn to the introductory tune......

"Oh we are all the friends of Jesus, we're all the friends of God;

We're trying to live as honest Christians in the way the Saints have trod..."

The resultant publicity resulted in a short slot on BBC Nationwide, and a plethora of correspondence, most asking for a copy for the words, and a few denouncing me for 'bastardising' Christian worship. Hot on the heels of the 'Match of the Day' hymn, I wrote a seasonal one, "Purple is the Colour, Advent is the Name....." set to the tune of the Chelsea Football song. At least the choirboys enjoyed it!

The Youth of the Parish

As there had been virtually no facilities for the young people of the parish, the official Youth Club in the village catering only for the official youth aged fourteen to twenty-one, I decided to set up a club for post-confirmees. Confirmation training had involved them in a six-month course of preparation and Sunday worship; after the confirmation they found themselves in something of a vacuum. So the 'Border Club' came into being, it being sited, geographically on the boundary between the two civil parishes of Ruscombe and Twyford. The name was a diplomatic coup. The minimum age for the confirmation at this time was twelve, a group for whom there was no recreational provision, and so the new club was welcomed by youngsters and parents alike. Each year, we added the next batch of young people – about fifteen to twenty each year. I had to make sure that the club didn't 'grow up' alongside the eldest members, and always bore in mind the needs of the whole group. We had a varied programme of entertainment, recreation and information, from trampoline practice in the Vicarage garden, to film shows, 'Fish 'n' Chip rambles – which involved ordering before setting off, and then meeting 'the supper' half way round the ramble. We also used to go swimming at the local Roman Catholic Convent, ice skating at Richmond in London, and watching stock car racing at Aldershot. On one ice skating trip, one of the young girls broke her ankle, but didn't tell me about it until we were back on the minibus, heading for home. I had no option but to call in at Ascot hospital on our way back, and leave her there overnight; I then had to explain it all to her parents who were waiting at the Vicarage to collect her on our return. They were very understanding; these were the days before the benefit of mobile phones. I eventually became quite adept at driving a minibus, though we did have one or two close shaves! We also raised quite a lot of money for charity; the highlight of our annual fundraising was an eleven mile sponsored walk around Windsor Great Park during which we raised over a thousand pounds for 'Action Research for the Crippled Child' over five years. We held Disco's – with an attendance of over one hundred young people and their guests; we kept a weather eye out for alcohol, and despite all our efforts, found ourselves sweeping up empty beer bottles at the end of the evening. Luckily, it was in the days before drugs. Controlling such numbers was not without its difficulties; on one occasion, I refused a bunch of older boys' entrance to the function - experience told me they were potential trouble-makers. When the time came to go home, I discovered they had wreaked retribution by slashing all four tyres on my car, parked around the back. On another occasion, I went out to sort out an argument between two groups of lads, and as a result was threatened with a metal comb – I survived, though, unscathed.

Working holidays

It was during our time at Twyford that I started doing 'locum' work in order to get a break. With three small children, there was no way we could afford a proper holiday, so during the school holidays I arranged to go down to Kent, to look after someone else's parish for three weeks, doing only Sunday services, and any emergency visiting and funerals. We had previously tried this type of summer break to advantage for a fortnight at Boreham Wood, and it had worked fine. Now it was the turn of the parishes of Sellinge, Stowting and Monk's Horton in Kent to suffer my ministrations for three weeks. The vicar there had kindly closed Monk's Horton for the period of our stay, so I only had the remaining two churches to service during our holiday. The routine was to celebrate an 8.00 a.m. service of Holy Communion at Sellinge, the main church of the group, where the vicarage was situated and in which we were staying; then a quick breakfast, and off the few miles to Stowting for a 9.15 a.m. said Communion; back to Sellinge for Matins at 11.00 a.m., and then the rest of the day free until Evensong at 6.30 p.m. On the first Sunday we were there, I dashed off to Stowting in good time for their service, arriving at about 9.00 a.m. I prepared the altar, the vestments and the bread and wine. By 9.15 a.m. no-one had appeared. At 9.20 a.m. in came one of the churchwardens. I asked if anyone else was coming, and was told that they'd be along at about twenty-five past the hour. And so they did. And so I started. A few more trickled in, and by 9.40 a.m. I had a full complement of at least twenty.

Word must have got around during the following week that I was a stickler for time and punctuality, because the following Sunday, most of the congregation were in their pews by 9.20 a.m. The following Sunday they were all in their pews by 9.10 a.m. ready for me to start on time. I was impressed. However, on our return home after the holiday I received a formally polite thank you letter from the vicar, in which he concluded, "On the Sunday I took up duties again in Stowting, I arrived, as usual, in church at 9.25 a.m. to find the whole congregation ready and impatiently waiting. What did you do to achieve that?" I cannot help feeling that my time-keeping habits eventually brushed off on their vicar!

Some years later, we were to take 'proper' holidays, many of which were adventures into France, to the beaches of Brittany, and as far down the west coast as Royan. Ecumenically, they were an eye opener; the amount of participation Anglicans were allowed in Roman Catholic services in this country was minimal; basically, you could witness the Mass, but not much else. On our first visit to France, I approached the Curé and asked his permission to attend Mass the following day. He not only welcomed me to his church, but invited me to receive the sacrament as well. Oh, if only all Roman Catholic churches were so broadminded!

Ecumenism and the Roman Catholic congregation

When I first arrived in Twyford, there existed a Roman Catholic congregation who had no church building. Their Sunday Mass was held in an ancient Nissen hut which had, over the years had a multiplicity of uses. It proved not to be a popular building for worship, as it stank of stale beer and cigarettes after each previous Saturday evening's merrymaking.

However, there existed in the two villages a tremendous community spirit, and this was channelled each year by a somewhat zealous Anglican layman into an annual fund raising venture for Christian Aid. Derek Barnes, well known within all three Christian denominational congregations was no respecter of church divisions, and motivated all the local organisations (of which there were many) together with the three churches into a frenzied week of fund-raising activities, along with a highly organised house-to-house collection. Scouts, Guides, Brownies and Cubs, all three local primary schools, women's, men's and sporting organisations, youth fellowships – all were cajoled into a diversity of fund-raising activities in the common aim. On the Monday following Christian Aid Week, we all used to gather in the hall of the Congregational Church for the big 'count-up', when a tally board was erected, and the house-to-house offering envelopes were opened, emptied and counted. I still remember the round of applause and great cheer that met the announcement, the year we first raised over a thousand pounds during the week. After that, each successive year presented the challenge to beat the previous year's total – and this the villages did for about ten years. It was always a challenge to devise new and exciting events year on year – and we never failed to raise thousands of pounds. The whole extravaganza was monitored by a Committee comprised of the three denominational clergy, and two representatives from each of the three churches. I mention this only because the existence of this committee was to have a profound effect on the ecumenical life of the community. From these humble ecumenical beginnings stemmed the creation of a far more widely reaching inter-church group – the Twyford and Ruscombe United Christian Council. This was the first case I had ever experienced of the child creating the parent Committee. It was this parent group, the United Christian Council that gradually made itself responsible for all the inter-church co-operation in the villages – joint and united services on Remembrance Sunday, the Good Friday Procession of Witness and courses of joint study during Lent each year. Not only did the existence of this

Council foster good relationships between the three churches, it also enabled Christians of differing denominations and outlooks to begin to take on board some of the prejudices which until then had kept them apart. Two 'ecumenical' occasions highlight the differences in discipline between the three churches. On the first occasion, the ecumenical United Christian Council needed funds. Louis Catterall, the Roman Catholic priest got out his cheque book, and immediately wrote out a cheque. As the Anglican priest present, I told the meeting that I was *certain* that my PCC would agree to an equivalent sum. The United Reformed Church Minister informed the meeting that he would put the request to his Church Meeting; he *hoped* that they would agree to give the required amount.

On another occasion, we were planning an ecumenical event, and were trying to recruit church members to 'come along on the Saturday morning' to help with cutting the grass. A couple of Anglicans volunteered; a couple of non-conformists also agreed to help, and the influential Roman Catholic member on the Committee without a second thought, kindly offered to 'send his gardener' to assist. What a world we lived in!

One of the most significant outcomes of this ecumenical co-operation was the understanding which developed between myself and the local Roman Catholic priest – a very easy going Irishman. As we grew together in friendship so it became obvious to me that there was one, further significant step which needed to be taken. I broached it informally first with Louis Catterall. At that time, they had no premises of their own, and were celebrating a Sunday Mass in this almost derelict, ancient village Hall. Since our Sunday Communion service at Ruscombe was over each Sunday morning at 9.45 a.m., how would they feel about using our church for their Mass each Sunday at 10.15 a.m. I wondered? He was overjoyed at the prospect, so I approached the Bishop to check out on the legalities of the idea, and then put it to the P.C.C. My P.C.C. Treasurer at that time was an Irish Protestant, and I feared he would lobby a negative vote – but much to my amazement, he didn't. The Church Council was very much in favour of the proposal, with one condition – no incense was to be used. And so it came to be – the most amicable of arrangements – the Roman Catholic Mass following on the tail end of the Anglican Communion Service, Sunday by Sunday. The only confusion arose on the two Sundays in the year at the beginning and end of summertime. There were always some parishioners who forgot to alter their clocks and watches the night before – and so it became a regular occurrence for Anglicans to turn up an hour late, in time for the Roman Catholic Mass, and at the other end of the year, for Roman Catholics to get up an hour early and find themselves joining an Anglican congregation! It was never intended to be a permanent arrangement, as the Roman Catholics were urgently raising funds for a church of their own, but for a period of several years it was a very happy, ecumenical understanding. Eventually their church was built, and a vast number of our Anglican folk attended the dedication of the new building. Eventually, when sufficient funds had been raised to pay off all the bills, the Bishop came to consecrate the new building, and we were again invited to be present, and to take part.

The sacrament of Confirmation

In England, I was still struggling in my own mind with the disciplines of the sacraments. As far as confirmation was concerned, I was happy; hardly anyone came forward to be confirmed other than of their own volition. Young people were certainly 'encouraged' by their parents, and sometimes pressured by their peer groups, but in confirmation preparation I always made two things quite clear from the start. I reserved the right, from the moment classes started, to cease preparing a candidate if I seriously considered they were not ready for the sacrament. Likewise, I also made it clear that any young person could come to me at any time, right up to the day before the service, if they felt that they themselves were not happy about going through with it. And this is exactly what happened. The group had been going strong for about five months, and we were nearing the end of the preparation classes. One particular boy, a slightly older lad, had been a 'star' pupil. On the night of the final class, after we had finished, he asked if he could stay behind to help me clear up. Not suspecting anything, I, of course, agreed. When everyone else had left, he said, "Can I ask you something?" "Yes" I replied, "What is it?" "I don't think I'm ready to be confirmed," he replied, "but I have a problem. You see, my mother and father have invited a whole load of relatives to the service tomorrow, and I know some of them have brought me presents; but I'm still not sure I'm ready to commit my life yet" "Do you want me to speak to your parents?" I asked him. "No, I must tell them myself. I just wanted you to know first. I'm sorry. I really appreciate all the time and energy you've spent, preparing us all, and it's been really interesting. And I will want to be confirmed, of that I'm sure, but just not yet". I was sad that he felt he couldn't go forward, but so pleased that he had had the courage and honesty to back out, even at the eleventh hour." He was confirmed, to my delight, two years later.

My other confirmation 'success' if you could call it that was at the other end of the age range. An elderly parishioner, dying of cancer, had been on my weekly visiting list for months. He was a cantankerous old codger, but we got on well together, and I think he appreciated my pastoral visits. One day, he asked about receiving the sacrament of Holy Communion before he died. I discovered that not only was he not confirmed, but that neither was he baptised and he was a Freemason to boot! I tried to explain to him the rudiments of Christian Initiation. Baptism, Confirmation and Communion. He claimed to be an agnostic, and asked why he needed Baptism and Confirmation as a pre-requisite to Holy Communion.

At that moment I had an inspiration. I asked him if I could be classed as a Freemason, if I hadn't subjected myself to instruction, and the initiatory rites of freemasonry. "Certainly not" he expostulated; *not before Initiation!*" He had to concur. I explained that Christianity was very similar – no initiation, no membership, no sacrament! Time was of the essence, and since we had already had long discussions on the rudiments of Christianity over several months, I felt that, in the circumstances, he could, and should be baptised without further delay. We managed to get him up to Ruscombe church one Sunday afternoon, and in the presence of his wife and the Verger he was baptised into the faith. The Confirmation Service was only a few weeks away, but even then, I wasn't sure he would live that long. But he was a determined gentleman, and he made it. I contacted the Bishop of Reading, and asked him if he would go with me to the house for a one-off, private confirmation, and also administer him his first communion. He was delighted to be able to do so, and it was a very meaningful and deeply spiritual service. He died only a few weeks later, after I had taken him the sacrament not more than three or four times.

The other memorable Confirmation Candidate was a young mother of thirty-seven. Two young teenage children, and one of five-and-a-half, she contracted breast cancer. It was a long drawn out affair, and I visited her regularly over several months in the Royal Berkshire Hospital. Towards the end, I visited her daily. She too asked to be confirmed, and as far as I was able, within the limitations of her periods of consciousness, I prepared her for the sacrament. The Bishop of Reading came to the hospital, Joyce was wheeled down to the hospital chapel, and there, in the presence of her ward sister, and two of her palliative care nurses she was confirmed on a hospital trolley, and received her first communion at the hands of the Bishop. She deteriorated rapidly after that, and I sat vigil with her day and night until she died. Her husband had stopped visiting her some weeks before; he couldn't cope with the pain of seeing her in hospital.

As I said, I did not have any problems with the sacrament of Confirmation, but I did have problems with the other two sacraments of Baptism and Marriage. Under the rules of the established church, I was obliged to baptise the children of any parents who came to me. I was young, high principled and naive. This concern had started much earlier, whilst I was in Bladon, but with so few baptisms during my time there, the pressure had hardly arisen. Now I was in a parish of several thousand people, and the baptism requests were coming in thick and fast. There seemed to be two mainstream practices in the Church of England; some clergy baptised all comers, willy-nilly, some even without any formal preparation, and others were much more discriminatory, applying all the 'rules' about residence, church attendance and the need for parents and god-parents to themselves be confirmed members of the church. Fat chance! Not only were god-parents more often than not, not confirmed, but also some parents weren't; some parents were not even baptised. But they still wanted their children 'christened'! Pressure was being put on them by *their* parents. On only one occasion did I refuse point blank to baptise an infant, when I discovered that the mother was a self-confessed Buddhist, and the father was a Muslim. However much I tried to convince them of the foolishness of their request, they still couldn't, or wouldn't see my reasoning. It was, to their mind, something that 'had' to be done. But not to mine – in the end, I didn't baptise their child. As they were not prepared to receive instruction in the Christian faith, I couldn't in all honesty baptise their child.

Overall, I took a middle line. I agreed to baptise all children, as long as least one parent was a baptised Christian. I used each approach as a pastoral opportunity, and gave every family as much preparation as I could before the ceremony. I also had an army of church members who followed up the families on the five succeeding anniversaries of their children's baptism. There was a major benefit to this policy. I discovered that, over a period of years, my early ministrations were leading to several adults coming forward for Confirmation (in some cases necessitating adult baptism) as a result of the pastoral care they had received over the baptism of their children.

Christian Marriage

Marriage was my other pastoral and spiritual stumbling block. Again, in those days, by law, I was obliged to marry all comers, as long as one of the parties to the marriage had a residential qualification, or was a regular attender at church services, and was a baptised Christian. Both parties to the union had to be of single status; church rules dictated that divorcees could not be married in church, even if one party to the marriage claimed to be the 'innocent' party.

How times have changed! Sadly, the church's rules were wide open to all sorts of mis-interpretations. What was a 'residential' qualification? A suitcase left at an auntie's house? What, I asked myself, did Christian marriage mean to those who had been baptised as infants, and had not darkened a church's doors since? I used to insist that couples came to church at least three times before their wedding, to 'hear the Banns read'. It was the custom, before I came to the parish, for relatives to take on this duty. But I insisted; I felt it gave the couples at least a fleeting acquaintance with the church prior to their wedding. And I was rigorous with marriage preparation. A long preliminary interview when they came to arrange the date, and either one or two subsequent interviews to discuss the ramifications of Christian marriage, and the implications of the words of the service itself. I was never happy when couples arrived at the vicarage and said, "We've fixed the date of our wedding reception, can you marry us on the fourteenth of next month at 3.00 p.m.?" Diplomatically, I let it be known around the parish that a visit to the Vicar to arrange the date of the wedding was the *first* priority, despite the difficulties of arranging a reception to match. It worked. However, I still had to deal with what I can only describe as 'godless' marriages. Services at which members of the congregation came into church well the worse for drink. Occasions when I found members of the congregation stubbing out their cigarettes in the porch. On one occasion I even had to stop one young man lighting up a cigarette in church! Many didn't join in the service; some didn't know how or when. Each of these services was a challenge to my ingenuity. I was still, at that stage, trying to exercise my ministry by the 'rules' of the church. Little by little I came to realise that the 'rules' weren't written for the real church and its wayward members, but rather for a non-existent ecclesiastical utopia.

I shall never forget the day at Twyford Church when, at the altar rail during the administration of the sacraments, I found myself in front of three young men who obviously didn't know what to do. They were looking around, to see what everyone else was doing. I had always been taught that it was wrong to administer the sacrament to those not confirmed. On the other hand, there were differing traditions in the broad-band church, and it could have been that either they hadn't been to church for ages, or were from some other branch of the church. I couldn't take a chance. I put the wafer bread in their hands, at the same time saying a silent prayer to the Almighty, "If they're not confirmed, Lord, forgive me!" After the service, they stood outside, waiting for a word with me. Nervously and in a faltering voice, they pushed one of them forward and said, "Vicar, my brother has something to ask you." "O.K." I replied brightly, "What is it?" "I want to get married." he said, hesitantly. I was forced to ask the £64,000 question. "Are you a confirmed member of the church?" He looked back blankly; obviously the question meant nothing to him. I tried again. "Are you a Baptised member of the Church" I asked. "No, he replied as he looked at his two brothers, "none of us are baptised. Does it matter?" I explained as briefly as I could that it did, unless his fiancée was baptised. "Oh yes, she's baptised, I'm almost sure," he replied. I made a date for them to come and see me during the week, and all was well; my conscience was clear (except for the communion incident!) They were married later that summer.

Finally, whilst on the subject of weddings, I must record the story of one of the strangest, and yet most deeply spiritual and moving weddings I was ever asked to solemnise. It was held in Twyford Church, a gaunt, three-hundred-and-fifty-seater building. There were only five of us at the service, the bride, the groom, the bride's and the groom's best friends, and me. On a midweek morning – no hymns – just the statutory wedding service with a short address and the prayers and blessings. The bride gave herself away to her husband, and their friends were the witnesses, as required by law. They were orphans, both of them, with no family on either side. They were going out to Africa to do Voluntary Service Overseas [VSO] on the following day. They wanted to go out there married, and with God's blessing on their union. I have conducted hundreds of weddings during my active ministry: some of them huge, important occasions, others rowdy, noisy affairs; even services for members of my own family – but never a service like the one I conducted on that Wednesday morning. It was a truly memorable occasion.

Funerals and Burials

And finally, though not a sacrament, this story would not be complete without a paragraph or two on that other troublesome area of a parson's life, Christian burial and funerals.

During the course of my parochial ministry, I have had endless problems with undertakers; they seemed to consider that they were a law unto themselves, and that the clergy were employed by them to do their bidding. Over the years, with I believe a pervading influence emanating from the United States, they had achieved and attained an influence and authority which they then exercised over most, if not all of their 'clients' and clergy alike. Logistically, the sheer number of parishioners for which we were pastorally responsible meant that, unlike in the old days, where each tiny parish had its own parish priest, who knew everybody and who all knew him, it was just not possible, neither to know about every single death that occurred in the parish, nor to be aware of every case of serious illness. The result was that, when a parishioner died, unless they were known as regular churchgoers and had received pastoral visits, the first person their relatives contacted was the undertaker —or 'Funeral Director', as they preferred to be called – another American innovation. They then discussed the funeral options between themselves without any reference to the priest who would be officiating, deciding not only the location of the funeral Service - in church or at the Crematorium - but also the preferred date. Then and only then did the undertaker offer to phone the incumbent on their behalf to make the final arrangements. This suited the relatives down to the ground; it saved them the embarrassment of having to contact their vicar, whom they either did not know or had never met, and about whom they felt a great sense of guilt, as they were now asking for his services although they had rarely, if ever darkened the church's doors. So the undertaker (I refuse to pander to their sense of aggrandisement by referring to them by their preferred American title) would then telephone me and say something after the manner of, "Vicar – a Mrs Jones/Smith/Evans has died; I don't know if you knew her, or even of her. I've been in touch with the family, and they would like the service next Thursday at the Crematorium at 3.30 p.m. If you are unable to take the service on this day and at this time, we can always get the 'duty chaplain'." This totally denied me, as their parish priest, the opportunity of any bereavement counselling. If the date already chosen was not convenient to my diary, it was embarrassing to ask the relatives to change it to a mutually convenient date to suit us both. With the undertaker having already 'arranged' with the family to hold the service at the crematorium (this, simply because it saved them the double journey to the church and them on to the crematorium, and so it took them less time and less man hours) it was almost impossible to 'undo', and replace the arrangements with a proper funeral in church, followed by cremation. We, the clergy were being undermined by the close knit brotherhood of undertakers, with whom I crossed swords on many occasions.

The worst memory of all concerned a cot death in my parish. I was telephoned very early one morning by a totally distraught young mother, whose baby had died during the night. She was distressed enough at the fact of the death; she was even more distressed by the undertakers crass questioning and subsequent statement. "Had their baby been baptised?" "No?" "In that case," he continued to the parents, "it couldn't be buried in consecrated ground!" I dropped everything and rushed down to the house. I ejected the undertaker, and then began the job of consoling and reassuring the parents. I assured them that of course their baby could be buried in the churchyard, and that the undertaker was totally wrong in his application of an ancient, ecclesiastical belief that the churchyard was a prohibited area to the 'un-baptised'. This incident led to major discussions between myself and the local undertakers as to correct ethical practice; I had been unhappy for some time by the way in which we, the clergy were being 'dictated to' and coerced into fitting in with their arrangements. Our discussions led to a new understanding between us, and made all the local undertakers far more wary in all our future dealings. Another milestone had been achieved in re-establishing the place of the church in the life of the parish.

I have already mentioned that in some respects I was living, and ministering on the very edge of the church as far as what was legal was concerned; luckily it was during this period in my ministry that the church rescinded its strict rules on who was, and who wasn't eligible to receive the sacrament of Holy Communion. Under Canon B17(a), Holy Communion was finally allowed to be administered to 'Confirmed Anglicans, and those of other Christian Denominations who were in good standing in their own churches'. Funnily enough, when this relaxation of the rules was put to the PCC for discussion and agreement, the most vociferous opponent, subsequently over-ruled, was a member of the Methodist Church who hadn't previously informed me of his denomination, and who had been receiving the sacrament for years!

The Parish and Mission

One of the annual highlights of our parish life was the 'Missionary Weekend'. Every year in mid-summer, I used to invite a 'working' missionary who was 'home on furlough' to visit the parishes, staying at the Vicarage over the weekend, and joining in Parish life, preaching, and sharing informally with members of the congregation and the parish as occasion allowed. The first time I wrote to a Missionary Society - U.S.P.G. – The United Society for the Propagation of the Gospel – they tried to send me a senior member of their London staff; however, I insisted that I wanted someone fresh from the mission field, with up-to-date accounts of the church overseas.

Among the memorable visitors whose company we enjoyed was the Bishop of Chota Nagpur, the Right Reverend Sadanand Abinash Bisram Dilbar Hans, an aborigine, a tribal Bishop from North India. I collected him from a neighbouring parish one Thursday evening, and brought him home to the vicarage for supper. I had a reasonable programme prepared for him; a visit to the local church Infant School on the Friday morning, a meeting with parishioners on the Friday evening, the parish garden Party on the Saturday afternoon, and three Sunday services, including an informal get-together on the Vicarage lawn after evensong, at which church people could ask questions about his church and his work. He had already visited several parishes in the rural deanery by the time he came to us, so I suggested a quiet Thursday evening, resting at the Vicarage. All he wanted to do was watch television!. To him it was a miracle – a novelty; even when we moved to the dining room for supper, he asked for the set to be left on, and to be able to sit facing the set! Although Jill and I were normally selective about our viewing, Bishop Hans insisted on the TV being left on right up to the time when I switched it off after the final National Anthem, and he had watched the little white dot disappear off the screen. Trying to discuss the next day's programme was extremely difficult – his mind was elsewhere most of the time!

The following morning we set off for the school. I must explain that the population of Ruscombe and Twyford were for the most part typically 'white' Caucasian – the only ethnic minorities were the families of the local Chinese Take-Away restaurant, so it was quite a novelty for the children of the infants' school to be introduced to an Indian Bishop. He endeared himself to the children, the staff and me with the delightful story he proceeded to tell. He made no apology for his colour. He asked the children if they knew why he was the perfect, rich brown colour that he was, and when they replied in the negative, he told them this story. I've never forgotten it.

"When God first made the world", he said, "there were no people on it at all. And God thought to himself, 'We really must have some people', but he had never made people before. So he took some earth, and some water, and made some people - rather like we make gingerbread men, and he laid them out in rows to dry in the sun. Later, when he came back, he discovered to his horror that they had turned black. They were overdone - not a very good colour, so he put them in Africa. He tried again. He made some more people, put them out in the sun, and thought to himself, 'I must come back sooner, before they burn. So he did... ...but when he returned, they weren't brown enough, they had a whitish/pinkish hue. They're not much good either, he said to himself, so he put them in England. And then he tried again. He made some more people in the same way. And he put them out in the sun, just as he had done with the other two groups. He decided not to give them as much sun as the first lot, but more than the second. He came back, and lo and behold - they were *perfect*. A beautiful, rich, dark, chocolate brown. Absolutely perfect! So he put them in Chota Nagpur! And that" he said to the children, "is why I am this perfect colour brown. All the best brown-coloured people live in Chota Nagpur!!"

The Garden Party on the Saturday was a great success. The Bishop entered fully into the spirit of the day, taking part in the games and competitions, and talking freely to everyone. That was one of the features of our annual vicarage 'do' – it attracted both church and non-church people; the parents of our Sunday school children, the fringers, the family service less frequent attenders, and the curious. The Bishop took them all in his stride, though secretly I felt he might have preferred to have been sitting in the sitting room, watching television! One of my firm rules [with the agreement of the P.C.C.] was that all the proceeds of every annual Garden Party should be given to the mission of the visiting missionary. I'm sure this well published fact contributed to the generosity of all present, and the final gift to the Bishop was much appreciated.

Coming as he did from a particularly poor area of India, he was quite overwhelmed.

I had gone to considerable lengths to discover from U.S.P.G. Head office the form of Communion used in Chota Nagpur, so that we could have a celebration of Holy Communion by the Bishop using a Rite with which he was familiar. Having obtained what I was told was the appropriate service, my secretary and I had spent hours before the Bishop's arrival, typing, duplicating, collating and stapling some sixty copies of the order of service for the members of the congregation. During supper on the Saturday evening, I proudly presented a copy of the service, with a view to finalising which parts of the service each of us would do. He took one look at the results of our labours and burst out laughing. I asked him what was so funny. He said, "We haven't used *this* service for years – we use the Church of England Book of Common Prayer!" Well, I did *try* to make him feel at home!

The services on the following day were again not only well attended, but much appreciated. At the end of Evensong on the Sunday night, I asked the Bishop to pronounce the blessing in his native tongue, which he was happy to do. We then 'repaired' to the vicarage lawn for coffee and an informal gathering. One elderly lady of the evening congregation took me on one side to voice her disquiet. "Are you sure," she asked, "that that was a *Blessing* that the Bishop gave at the end of the service? It could have been absolutely anything! It could have been a curse! You just never know, do you!'" I reassured her that the Bishop was a man to be trusted, and, I think, allayed her fears.

The other well remembered missionary who came for one of our 'weekends' some years later, towards the end of my time there, was a woman priest. This was well before the subject of the ordination of Women, or even their legality had even been mooted in Synod. Joyce Bennett had been ordained in Hong Kong as part of the Church there. She had been working as a missionary for C.M.S. [the Church Missionary Society] and was on furlough during the time that I was looking for another 'visiting' missionary. She happily agreed to come. For the benefit of the reader, I must perhaps explain that as the church was divided between 'High' and 'Low' – parish churches and the Theological Colleges, so too were the Missionary societies. U.S.P.G. was an 'Anglo-Catholic' society, C.M.S. was Evangelical. So Joyce Bennett was from the evangelical wing of the church. By the time she came to our parish, both Ruscombe and Twyford churches were of one mind, and were 'moderate' in churchmanship, although we still retained vestments for the Eucharist, but not much other ritual or ceremonial. Joyce arrived on the Thursday evening as was the pattern, and settled in at the Vicarage. The same system obtained; a visit to the school on the Friday morning, a visit to the Mother's Union on the Friday afternoon, the Garden Party on the Saturday and three services on the Sunday. However, it was, as I remember, Trinity Sunday – the Sunday for white vestments. I should have been more sympathetic to her churchmanship. [or church*woman*ship, I suppose!] but I did actually ask her, for the people's sake, to wear vestments with which they were familiar. She magnanimously agreed. I invited her to share the altar with me at both communion services, and to con-celebrate. This was way outside the 'rules' obtaining at the time, but by now in my ministry, I was forging ahead, taking the people along many, uncharted waters! Joyce agreed, and so for the two morning communion services, we used the white vestments from both Ruscombe and Twyford Churches. It was a deeply significant occasion – standing at the altar sharing in the words of consecration with in my opinion, a quite legitimately ordained woman priest at my side. What I didn't realise until after the service at Twyford was that inadvertently we were more than united by sacrament – we were united by vestment. The two white sets of vestments were decorated differently, and in our haste to get vested between the services, we had intermingled the various vestments – a memorable, liturgical unity!! Of course it didn't matter one whit – but it was fun to become aware of it, after the service!

Outside Twyford Church with the Revd. Joyce Bennett, OBE., of the Church Missionary Society during a 'Missionary Weekend'.

A Musical Adventure

Still on the ecumenical scene, it was at about this time that I found myself involved in a musical adventure, which was to move my 'churchmanship' forward another couple of notches. Although I had become much more broad-minded over the course of two curacies, I was still what might be termed a moderately catholic Anglican; the differentials are far more blurred now that they were then, but the three 'orders' of churchmanship were still fairly identifiable. A High Church Anglican was one using vestments, wearing a biretta when out in the street, and who still used the Roman Missal as their Prayer Book for 'the Mass'. In the centre-ground were the Prayer Book Catholics, sticking to the rubrics of the Book of Common Prayer, and wearing either Vestments or surplice and stole at 'The Eucharist' or 'Holy Communion'.

And then at the lower end of the scale were the evangelical group – identifiable by their use of extempore prayer, a dislike of all forms of vestments, and who wore 'choir robes' [cassock, surplice or gown and scarf and academic hood], and celebrated Holy Communion or 'The Lord's Supper' from the north end of the Holy Table. No altar for them! In brief, you could say, perhaps that the High Church element emphasised the Sacraments, and the 'Low' Church the Preaching of the Word'. I sincerely believed that both were an appropriate part of the Christian life, and so my churchmanship was somewhere in the middle. I practised an accurate use of the Prayer Book, with a certain reluctance to diverge from the printed word; I was unfamiliar with the practice of 'extempore' prayer but happy to write appropriate prayers where the prayer book fell short, or was found to be lacking. I was happy with the use of vestments, surplice and stole, or surplice, hood and scarf, whatever happened to be the tradition wherever I was, and my tendency was to write out all my sermons in full, word-for word, but then to refer to them only as a guide to keep my thoughts focussed. I was unable, at that time, to preach 'extempore'.

And so it was that I was introduced to an American musical, gospel and evangelistic experience. A friend of mine had acquired the long-playing record of the score of "Come Together" a musical with biblical words arranged by two American evangelists, Jimmy and Carol Owens. The 'oratorio' is almost impossible to describe. The words are scriptural, the intervening 'encouragements' are typically what you might expect from 'across the pond', and the whole work was totally absorbing and inspirational, even to a die-hard, established Anglican priest! A group of us played the record over and over again. The tunes were catchy, and before long we were all joining in the choruses.

It appeared that this 'musical' was soon to be performed in Reading Town Hall. A group of us attended, not knowing quite what to expect. It was certainly an eye-opener for me. It gave me my first experience of 'praying in the Spirit' and 'Praying in tongues'. We split up into groups for personal prayer time, and our group was led, I remember, by a zealous little man in a sharkskin pale blue suit. We 'huddled' in a close-knit circle rather like a rugger scrum, and he started to pray – with us, and for us; then he invited us to 'join in'. I was dumb-struck. I felt uneasy – it was right outside my experience. The prayers came to an end, and the 'musical' re-started. The words haunt me to this day, as do the tunes. 'Come together, in Jesus' name. He is here; he is moving among us. Clap your hands, all you people. (this, an 'action' song). I'd never clapped at a worship service before, but it seemed the most natural thing in the world to do. "Hallelujah, his blood avails for me,. I once was lost, and now I'm found; was blind but now I see." Words from the traditional doxology. 'Praise God from who all blessings flow..." Another short but so easily remembered chorus – "Freely, freely you have received, freely, freely give....." A long exhortation, spoken *over* background music – again, a totally new phenomenon, but it worked so well. "Blest be the tie that binds our hearts in Christian love.. "as we all joined hands, and exchanged a 'kiss' of peace. (Another totally new experience.) Very tactile – not any part whatsoever of the Anglican tradition. I was hooked ! The penitential section, "All we like sheep have gone astray..." and the 'absolution from St. John's gospel, chapter 3, verse 16. "God so loved the world that He gave His only begotten Son..." And then the grand finale – and I challenge anyone not to be moved by those words from the Book of the Revelation of St. John the Divine, spoken over a rising crescendo of music, working to a climax. "Blessing, and honour, and glory and power be unto God and to the Lamb, for ever and ever." Words alone cannot even begin to describe the spiritual experience of the occasion. As I say, we were hooked! It was so outside anything previously experienced, and yet it touched places in our hearts that even Heineken could never have begun to reach! It significantly changed my spiritual outlook, it significantly changed my life.

'Come Together' was sweeping across the countryside like an evangelistic Christian plague. A group of us travelled to Surbiton, to Ewell Technical College in Surrey, and to Southwark Cathedral, during which time we were rehearsing a truly eclectic group of musicians and singers drawn from all denominational churches in both Wokingham and Twyford. Our 'moment of glory' came when we launched ourselves upon an unsuspecting public, first at Wokingham, in the parish church, and then at Loddon Hall – the Community Centre in Twyford – in February 1975.

Whilst we had been busy preparing to perform locally, we were at the same time attending performances of the sequel – "If My People..."and just as soon as we had concluded 'Coming together' we started a whole new round of rehearsals, whilst at the same time gaining experience by travelling to the Albert Hall, to the Westminster Hall in London, to Chidrey near Wantage and to Nettlebed near Henley-on-Thames to witness and participate in this new work by Jimmy and Carol Owens.

It was just as inspirational, just as moving – and this time we forsook the previously secular venue, and performed it in Twyford Church. The place was packed to the walls – it was 'standing room only' – and the atmosphere was electric. I believe it to be true that several people had their lives changed by these performances in Twyford and Wokingham, and although people didn't fill the churches to bursting point every successive Sunday, I am convinced the end result was an envigorated church within the community. Some of the choruses from both works have now been adopted by several 'modern' hymn books as standard Sunday fare.

The presentation of the Jimmy and Carol Owens' musical "If my People..." performed in St. Mary's Church Twyford.

The Parish Church and the local Schools

Another aspect of my ministry that was in fact most rewarding, but that went for the most part unknown and unrecognised was my involvement in the life of the local schools. For my sins, I was elected or co-opted onto the governing bodies of all the four schools that served the community. I became closely involved in the life of the local Infant school, as it was a Church school. Whereas my involvement didn't go as far as a regular, weekly teaching slot, I was a very regular visitor, frequently taking morning assemblies – one of my strengths – and was involved on a regular basis in the appointment of teaching staff. My greatest joy, however, was the close liaison with which I was blessed with the State Primary School at the furthest end of the village. The headmaster was a committed agnostic, but we got on very well together, and I became a regular visitor to the school, taking small groups in religious and moral education, and attending all their school functions – Carol Services at Christmas, Sports Days, end-of-term concerts and all the other main morning assemblies. The children were always very welcoming, and we enjoyed a good rapport – children and staff alike. I was also privileged to serve on the governing bodies of the 'State' Junior School, and the Church of England Secondary School. I shall never know just how much my steadying influence affected the decision making on their respective governing bodies, but I like to think that in some small way I brought a sense of Christian values to the attitudes of the more secular members of those groups.

Parish Finance

One of the problems with an ever changing population and therefore, congregation was the need for a system of regular funding. Apart from the 'quota' or Parish Share paid annually to the diocese, to offset their costs of incumbents stipends, diocesan administrative staff and other expenses, we had two large and expensive church buildings to maintain, as well as a somewhat decrepit Church Hall (a former Church School), honoraria to pay a limited parish staff, and other maintenance and running costs. I decided that, with the consent of the PCC, we would run a "Stewardship Campaign". At that time, my experience was limited to the similar one which had been held in my former parish of Redditch, and so, upon this pattern we launched our giving initiative. This involved employing a professional team of stewardship fund-raisers, and gathering together two teams of parishioners – an army of church womenfolk, responsible for inviting families to a 'Grand Supper', for arranging suitable baby-sitters and a crèche for the evening, and acting as hostesses on the night. Following the supper, each attending invitee, (and later, the absentees) were visited in their own homes, and invited to make regular and realistic contributions to the funding of their church.

The Family

During these eighteen years of a developing ministry, my three daughters were growing up, and moving from school to school. As they got older, Jill, my wife was able to take up her teaching career again, and although it came as a shock to me, my daughters began gradually to grow away from the church. Rachel, our youngest, attending a private school in Reading, attached herself for a while to an evangelical, Anglican Church in Reading attended by many of her school friends. Sarah, our middle daughter, who for a period, attended a Roman Catholic school in Slough, made a similar break with our parish church, and joined an evangelical 'house' church in Maidenhead, which had no building of its own, and worshipped on Sunday mornings in Maidenhead Public Library. She regaled us with accounts of the vast amounts of money raised by 'tithes', which her church was giving away to support Christian work overseas. I had to remind her that this was only possible because, unlike her father's church, there were no overheads involved, such as the on-going maintenance of two costly, historic buildings. It was at this point, I think, that I began seriously to realise just how much of the church's financial resources was being spent, nationally on 'plant' instead of on 'mission'. This utter 'in-balance' has aggravated me ever since, and the longer I have been in ministry, and the more near-empty churches it has been my misfortune to become aware of, the more painful has become this realisation.

I suppose it was only natural that in the course of time, my three daughters would flee the nest – not just from home, but from the strictures of a 'vicarage' upbringing. Which other children, I had to ask myself, were expected to be alongside their mother in the pew, every Sunday? And how irrelevant to teenagers were the services of the 1662 Book of Common Prayer? Even my more 'free-range' services, aimed at a younger congregation, fell far short of what I imagined worship should and could be like in the twentieth century. But I was still under the discipline of my 'ordinary' – my diocesan bishop - so my hands were more or less tied. I did what I could to bring our worship up to date – but it was not enough. As I came to realise later in my ministry, if urban churches are in some measure irrelevant to the spiritual needs of young people, how much more irrelevant are the worship practices of most of the churches in rural communities, which have hardly moved forward at all since the Reformation! And so it was that, in the April of 1985, we said goodbye to Twyford, and moved to Westmill in Hertfordshire. After a ministry lasting eighteen years, we were leaving behind a whole host of friends, as well as parishioners – it was an emotional time for us all.

Pronouncing the blessing at my final Eucharist Service at Twyford.

With my churchwarden George Roberts at my Farewell Party and Presentation at Twyford Junior School. (Courtesy of The Maidenhead Advertiser).

A gathering at Twyford of past clergy – The Revd. Herbert Hartley, the Revd. Graham Hamborg and myself, along with Rt. Revd. Richard Harries, Bishop of Oxford and John Redwood M.P for Wokingham.

Chapter 13

HERTFORDSHIRE -
WESTMILL & GREAT MUNDEN - 1986 - 1987

With all three of our children having grown through the primary and secondary school system (Sarah, our middle daughter having moved from the local C.of E. Secondary School to a Roman Catholic Secondary Convent School in Slough because of the attitude of her contemporaries towards her as a 'daughter of the Vicarage'), the time came to start considering an appropriate next move. I was, at that time, looking for a new challenge; it seemed somewhat pointless to me simply to exchange one large parish for another one, although I did realise (unlike some of my contemporary colleagues) how stale one could get staying in the same parish all one's active life. An incumbent who was priest in an adjoining parish when I was serving in Ruscombe and Twyford was still there some fifteen years later. It may have been a 'comfortable' parish for him – wealthy, well to do with a large, beautiful vicarage; it has certainly not done his parishioners any favours. They surely are entitled to some new blood, and some imaginative thinking, planning and preaching!

My next move - Hospital Chaplaincy or Christian Stewardship ?
Two alternative opportunities now presented themselves to me as possible 'career' moves. Taking up a hospital chaplaincy, or going into the Christian Stewardship movement. I started by offering myself for work with the former, but soon discovered it was very much a 'closed shop'. Hospital chaplains, it seemed 'bred' other hospital chaplains, and unless you had contacts with influence, getting a hospital job was well nigh impossible! Full-time chaplaincies were, it seemed, only offered to those clergy who had previously served as part-time chaplains; there was little hope of breaking into the 'system' – remunerative though it was – as I discovered, despite several job applications, and one or two unsuccessful interviews. One was in London, and the other at Stoke Mandeville, for which I was unsuccessful, due to the fact, which I later learned, of the Bishop of Reading's need to find an alternative position for a renegade priest from within the county. So I opted for my alternative choice – in no way a 'second string'. I was just as interested in the concept of Christian commitment and response as I was in a healing ministry. In this respect, I was much more successful. It was, for me, a 'transition' post; if it worked out, I could move on to full time Christian Stewardship; if it didn't, I could easily go back into full time pastoral ministry. I had had an interest in Christian Stewardship since those early days in Redditch, my first parish, and the 'Wells' Campaign to which my then Vicar had resorted, to boost rapidly depleting funds.

It was not long before an ideal opportunity arose – an advertisement in the

Church Times for a split post of Assistant Christian Stewardship Adviser in the Diocese of St. Albans, and priest-in-charge of two small country parishes. It was during this time that Jill had applied for and obtained a post as head of a brand new Nursery wing of a Primary School in Maidenhead; having had several part-time jobs in and around the area of the parish where we lived, and, now that our three young daughters were growing up, it was an opportunity to return to the fulfilling of her academic career, and a post for which she was well suited, and which she well deserved.

So I applied for the post of Assistant Christian Stewardship Adviser in the diocese of St. Albans; the only down side (and this was prevalent at the time) was the requirement to take responsibility as well for two small pastoral cures – as parish priest of two small country parishes in north Hertfordshire – the parishes of Westmill and Great Munden, along with the village of 'Nasty' – which sported only an evangelical 'Free' corrugated iron Church. The more I considered the job opportunity, the more it seemed appropriate.

So followed two interviews – one in the parish, and one at Diocesan Office, at which I was questioned on my stewardship experience and administrative skills. It took a few anxious days awaiting the result, and then a letter came from the Bishop, inviting me to take up the split post. At this point, Jill and I arranged a trip over to Westmill so see where we would be living; as it turned out, it was to be in an enormous, 19th century Vicarage with a huge, unmanageable garden. It was an architectural disaster of a house, with a grand central staircase, and not much else. It was to prove a difficult house to live in; it faced due east in an almost uninterrupted direct line to the North Sea, so was often beset by icy cold easterly winds which seeped into every nook and cranny of the ill-fitting windows. In addition, the walls were constructed of totally impermeable red brick, into which it was well-nigh impossible to drill holes for 'fixtures and fittings', even with a masonry drill. I well remember the day that, having erected shelving all along one complete wall of the study, and having finally completed unpacking all my books, the whole lot came cascading off the wall – shelves and all !

A hindrance in the Parish
By far the greater hindrance in the parish, though, was the 'senior' churchwarden, a retired Rear-Admiral. He ruled the parish like a Victorian forbear and 'Lord of the Manor'. No-one dared to speak at any meetings of the P.C.C., and out of deference, they all referred to him, and always addressed him as 'Admiral'. At my first meeting of the P.C.C., at which he called me by my Christian name, I replied using his. After the meeting, I was taken on one side by a senior member of the P.C.C. and told, "You should *never* refer to the Admiral by his Christian name – after all *he is "the Admiral"*. "Nonsense, "I replied, "if he is going to call me by my Christian name, I'm going to call him by his."

This decision marked a milestone in breaking down the master/serf relationship which had held sway in the village until that time; I like to think that this simple act brought about, over the next two or three years the beginning of a real sense of Christian community, and a breaking down of the old reserves, restrictions, limitations and mores. However, the relationship between the 'Admiral' and me were never quite the same again!

The other half of the post required acting as an assistant to the Diocesan Stewardship Adviser – a retired army major. Several advisers in the movement had taken up similar responsibilities after their retirement from the armed services. They tended to be died-in-the-wool, stuck-in-the-mud administrators with little or no visionary acumen, preferring the option of maintaining the status quo and doing as little 'active' work as the job allowed. As previously in my former parish life, I again found myself acting as the amanuensis – the dog's body – running the errands, visiting the parishes furthest from the office, and generally being the only one responsible (along with our departmental secretary) for any imaginative or visionary thinking. I was supposed to be 'trained on the job', but this consisted mainly of trailing around behind my 'boss' and watching him do as little as possible, using a scheme he had evolved right at the beginning of his time there. Suggesting changes was difficult – implementing them well nigh impossible.

However, I really enjoyed my time in the St. Albans diocese; I learnt quite quickly to keep my head down, and to do my own thing. For the most part, Rex Clarke the full time adviser was prepared for me to do just this. Working the two parishes of Westmill and Great Munden, however, was quite another matter. Apart from the 'admiral' trying to run the parish as a naval operation, the other point at which we came severely unstuck was in our totally differing views on liturgy and worship. As you will be aware, from what has gone before, I have, all my ministry, tried to be at the very cutting edge of liturgical reform. But whereas I respect those who hold the opposite view and adhere, lovingly to the ancient 1662 Book of Common Prayer, as a 'professional' I have always taken it upon myself to try to move the Church of England forward in all matters liturgical. Not so the 'Admiral'. He was a BCP (Book of Common Prayer) man through and through. Inevitably, therefore, it was destined that within a matter of a few weeks, we were likely to come to 'words' if not 'blows'!

One of the parish 'traditions', existing in the parishes before my arrival was the practice of the 'Admiral' and the churchwarden from my other parish meeting in church on each of the six week-nights – to say Evensong. My stewardship responsibilities made it impossible to attend many of these services, due to the fact that much of my work comprised attending evening meetings, many of them in outlying churches in the diocese, for which I had to leave early, having made a hasty tea. (During this time, Jill was still living in Maidenhead during the week, and coming home only at weekends and during the school holidays). This absence from church didn't go down at all well with the 'admiral', but on such occasions as I was able to be present, I reserved the right, as Rector of the parish, to 'say the office', using an updated version of the prayer book with which I had become well accustomed. The number of 'harrumphs' and snorts emanating from the other side of the chancel as the service unravelled were beyond counting. The admiral got his own back when reading the lessons, by using an antiquated, Authorised version of the scriptures!

However, my introduction of modernised forms of worship, and of 'Family Worship' once a month, involving children of the parish soon showed signs of an increasing interest in the church. Congregations grew, I opened up the church to class visits from the local school, introduced a new, modern hymnal and introduced lay participation during the services – intercessions as well as scripture reading – all well tried and tested practices which had proved themselves so successful in previous parishes.

The only real 'fly in the ointment' was the residence in the parish at that time of a former rector – a man well into his eighties - – the last Rector but one – much loved by some of the older parishioners for his subservience to the admiral, and his adherence to the Prayer Book of 1662. He had, apparently, been offered an almshouse in the parish by the chairman of the Almshouse Trustees – guess who? The Admiral!

This former rector was an affable enough sort of fellow, but never ceased reminding me of 'how things used to be in his time', and of the overwhelming merits of the Book of Common Prayer. The crunch came one morning, after we had both emerged from the church after saying Matins together, when as we walked down the village street one of the local children called out, "Good Morning, Rector!!" To this I replied, "Good Morning". I was not prepared for the response; "Not you, the other one."

Whereas Westmill Church was in the pastoral and geographical centre of the village, the church of Great Munden was on a country lane, apropos of nowhere in particular. Great Munden enjoyed one Holy Communion Service each Sunday morning, and Westmill a Holy Communion Service and an Evensong each Sunday. However, having had, in the olden days a vicar each they found it hard, not only to share a priest between the two churches, but also, and even worse, to have only a part-time priest, with diocesan responsibilities. The concept of change from a parish priest in his parish each and every day, to a priest on 'part time' duties and not always around, was the cause of some friction. This was despite the efforts of the Bishop, at my Installation, reminding a congregation of joint parishioners, that, as their priest, I would be "...in journeyings oft..." Parishioners, at least some of them, were determined to get their 'pound of flesh', and tried to demand more than their fair share of me; this, bearing in mind that with two parishes, two P.C.C.'s, and a full round of Sunday Services, Baptisms, Marriages and Burials, I could only allocate, at best, 25% of my time to each parish! Luckily, only one of the churches had a choir, and neither had a Sunday school, though I did take a weekly assembly at the local village school.

Difficulties at Great Munden
Several incidents covering the two parishes are well etched into my memory, not least at Great Munden, the parishioners of which decided to hold a fund-raising

event – an Arts and Crafts display and Flower festival in the church. I have no skills with flowers whatsoever, but in an attempt to show support for their endeavours, I called in at the church on the Friday morning prior to the Saturday festival. I have never seen so many strangers working so busily in the building. When I enquired from whence they came, I was told that they came from miles around; apparently it was a local tradition that everyone helped at *all* the churches in the area for most weekends, every summer. I gently suggested that it would be good to see them at the Sunday service the following day, to which I was given a shocked and horrified reply – they were only there to decorate the church; they rarely if ever attended a service! My horror was compounded when I went into the vestry to collect the registers for the following day. In the centre of the floor of my vestry was a bucket, and alongside the bucket was a roll of toilet paper! I thundered out of the vestry, demanding an explanation! It was another tradition, they explained – apparently they had never heard of the British tradition of *"... round the corner, behind the bush..."*. I removed the bucket forthwith, locked the vestry door, and forbade any flower decorator, on pain of death, to use my vestry as a lavatory, ever again. This might have seemed unreasonable, the church being remote from any public conveniences, but such was not the case in view of the fact that the chief flower decorator's house – that of the wife of the retired Major and PCC Treasurer was no more than one-hundred-and-fifty yards away. Apparently, she wasn't having them trampling all over *her* house to 'spend a penny'. The Churchwarden's house was even nearer still!

Meanwhile, at Westmill the Admiral continued to be a thorn in my flesh, taking every opportunity to undermine my authority, and subvert the congregation. On one occasion, he asked if I would allow the Baptism of the child of a distant relative in the parish church by a priest-friend of his from London. I explained that I, as the parish priest would be happy to perform the baptism, but that it really wasn't on to import both the baptismal party *and* the priest for what was basically a parish occasion. It was some months later – because we had very few Christenings in the parish, before I noticed in the parochial registers that, without any further reference to me, he had in fact arranged to have the Baptism carried out whilst I was away on holiday !!

Weddings
I remember, on one occasion, an upper class family in the parish (and great friends of the admiral and his wife) phoned me to arrange their daughter's wedding. I suggested, very politely to the bride-to-be's mother that if her daughter was old enough to get married, she was surely old enough to arrange her own wedding, and I made an appointment for the daughter and her fiancé to come to the Vicarage for a wedding interview (as had been my custom since I was first ordained.) The couple arrived, and things got off to a very bad start, with the bride informing me of the date she (or her mother!) had chosen for the wedding. It was my proven custom to discuss and agree mutually convenient

dates, but this opportunity was being denied me. Most unfortunately, the date the family had chosen was one that I just could not manage, as I had another appointment that day. "No matter", said the bride, your retired colleague can do it!" (Apparently, as it later turned out, this was what the family had had in mind all along, as the retired priest who lived in the parish was a long-standing family friend.) I reminded her that I was the Rector of the parish, and that we needed to find a *mutually agreeable* date. This was to prove an almost insurmountable hurdle, because by the time I was brought into the picture, the reception had been booked, along with a choir from London, cars, flowers, the lot! I stood my ground; the bride went into hysterics; I tried to calm her down, but to no effect, and the groom-to-be just stood helplessly around, unable to help or communicate at all. The couple returned home, and within seconds an irate mother-of-the-bride was on the telephone, berating me for upsetting her daughter, telling me just what she thought of me, and just what she intended to do about it. I explained, as best I could, that I was happy to go along with most of their arrangements, but that I was in fact the Rector, and was therefore pastorally responsible for *all* the services at the parish church.

Little did I realise, at that stage, just what I had let myself in for. For a country wedding in a small rural, Hertfordshire church, it was as if I was being asked to make arrangements for a wedding in St. Paul's Cathedral! I offered the services of the choir... and was politely told that a band of professional 'singers' –the 'Angel's Choir' from a London Church would be coming to sing. When I asked about the choice of entry and exit music and the hymns, I was told that there would be a contralto solo during the signing of the registers, and that one particular anthem would be sung by the choir alone. When I asked for the sheet music for this piece, so that the organist could practice it, I was told that it was only in manuscript form, and the composer was, at that time, on a trekking holiday in China! Then there were the flowers. I know from previous wide experience that mothers tend to go 'over the top' with their daughters' weddings, but this one really took the biscuit. Luckily, I happened to go into the church early on the morning of the wedding. I could hardly believe what I saw. The whole sanctuary was awash with floral tributes – there was nowhere to move, and certainly the siting of the arrangements left me no space for processing with the bride and groom, let alone any room for manoeuvre. Luckily, only the army of professional florists were present at that time, so, as politely and as firmly as I could, I asked for the positioning of them to be adjusted, to allow me entrance to, and egress from my own sanctuary. The florists readily agreed, commenting that they wondered when they had been given their instructions, just how I was going to manage. Sadly, just after the flower stands had been re-positioned, into church came... ...the bride's mother! She exploded! The florist kindly came to my support, explaining how I did need some space to conduct the ceremony. But the bride's mother was not a happy bunny! She had to concede that I had some say in how the church was decorated – and the positioning of the flower stands. Amongst the more bizarre requests from the bride's family was the suggestion that part of the churchyard fence be taken down, so that the wedding party and guests could walk directly from the church into their garden after the service. Once again, it was a request that I had to deny. The final problem came with the dictat that I wouldn't be taking the service at all; they had asked Gerald Hart to officiate! He was a former Rector of the parish, who had known the family previously, and had come back to live in a 'grace and favour' almshouse administered by my 'admiral' churchwarden. I explained to the bride's mother that, in fact, I was the Rector of the parish, and that I would be taking the ceremonies of the vows and promises at the service; I did however make the concession that Gerald Hart could lead the prayers and intercessions. Reluctantly, this was agreed.

There was even worse to come. Unknown to me, during the night before the wedding, Gerald Hart took an overdose of sleeping pills. The first I knew of this event was at about 9.30 a.m. the following morning, when the bride's mother telephoned me to inform me that Gerald Hart was dead, and that she had already contacted another nearby priest to perform those parts of the service which I had allocated to him. I could hardly believe my ears.

The service went off without a hitch – the 'Angels' choir were not much better than our resident village church choir, and the music that had been sent, post haste from China (or was it Tibet?) was nothing special either. What was far more incredible was that the death of the former Rector was 'hushed up' by the 'Admiral'. What had apparently happened was that when he hadn't appeared early the following morning, the admiral sent the husband of a choir member up a ladder to get into the almshouse to 'see what was wrong'. He found a bottle of tablets, empty on the bedside table, and Gerald Hart dead in bed. By the time the doctor had arrived, the tablet bottle had 'disappeared', the bed linen had been changed, and the doctor subsequently signed the death certificate as 'natural causes'. On the day before a family friend's daughter's wedding? I rest my case. I find such incidents very hard to rationalise.

The only other incident which is permanently etched on my mind whilst incumbent of the parish also concerned a wedding – this time of a regular villager. A simple rural family, who generously accepted all the help I could offer, and the suggestions I made. I was on familiar territory. I discussed the service with the young couple, and ascertained that all the ancillary arrangements – choice of hymns, service sheets, choir, cars, best man, bridesmaids and page-boys, ushers and wedding reception were all well in hand. We even arranged, without any fuss, an acceptable, mutually convenient date. Again, all went well until the morning of the wedding – as I remember it, it was a service scheduled for 2 o'clock in the afternoon. At about 9 a.m., I received a desperate telephone call from the bride's mother. Would I call down at the house without delay – they had a crisis on their hands! I duly arrived, somewhat mystified, and amid a cloak of secrecy was taken into the 'parlour'. An embarrassed mother-of-the-bride then informed me, in convoluted, round-about terms, that her younger, 14 year-old son, who was acting as 'chief usher' was in a state of hysterics. It had taken him some two hours to 'come clean' to his mother; apparently he had been experimenting with a piece of wire during the night in his bedroom, and had ended up with a piece of that wire, which had broken off, firmly embedded in his 'male member'. She wanted him to carry on as if nothing had happened until after the wedding, but he was in too much discomfort, and desperate with worry. What should she do? I arranged for a reliable member of the family with a car to take him to A&E at a nearby hospital. I reassured the bride's mother that all would be well, and that I was sure he would be back in good time. In fact, as it turned out, all was well; the hospital removed the offending piece of wire, and he returned to the village and the church duly subdued, just in the nick of time to perform his duties.

Jack of all Trades......

During my time in Westmill, I had the misfortune one summer, to break a bone in my ankle rather badly, which necessitated it being put in plaster for about two months. We had a large garden, mostly to grass – and it was couch grass, not an easily-tended lawn. Jill was working away all week, so could only attend to the garden at weekends. On one occasion I was hobbling around the front garden with plaster and crutches, when the admiral came calling. "Your lawn is a disgrace to the village" he remarked – "you ought to get it cut!" I was very tempted to suggest that as an act of charity, he might have offered his own services; as it was, I kept my own counsel.

Eventually the time came to look to the future. My period of 'split' ministry had served me well; I had tested my vocation in terms of a 'stewardship' ministry, whilst still maintaining an active participation in parish life. By this time, Jill had been offered and had taken up the post of head teacher of a brand new Nursery School in Royston, some six miles north of our parish. Now she could live at home, and enjoy our new found county. Sadly, the timing was disastrous. Not being aware at that time that my senior colleague in the diocese was seriously contemplating early retirement on medical grounds, I started to look for 'pastures new'. And I found them – again buried deep within the pages of the Church Times, an advertisement for a full-time Christian Stewardship Adviser in the Diocese of Hereford. Due to my early grounding in Indian history and Geography, I had only scant knowledge of the geography of the Welsh Marches, the West Midlands and the Wye Valley. My wife, who had only recently settled into her new home and teaching post, graciously agreed that we could move once again.

Although I had thoroughly enjoyed my many years in parochial ministry, despite all its ups and downs, I was now looking forward eagerly to a change in ministerial life-style, with new interests, greater freedom as my life approached retirement, and the many challenges that my new post would provide.

Chapter 14

HEREFORD - Sector Ministry - 1987 - 1999

So......I applied for the post, and with little opposition, was appointed. As a wordsmith, I was fascinated by the sign on the inside of the door of the Ludlow Conference Centre where we were billeted overnight during the interviews. Coming back from a 'swift half' at a local hostelry at about 10.30 p.m., we found the following cryptic notice affixed to the door; "Will the last one in please drop the catch!" Obviously someone with a sense of humour!

Because I was a priest, I was not permitted to have a 'lay' salary, or to purchase my own house. We were still obliged to live in a redundant 'grace and favour' vicarage. I had made it quite clear at interview that I planned to give 'a hundred and ten percent' to my Stewardship work, so would not be available as a 'part-time parish priest' as well. This was accepted and understood. Nevertheless, the diocese still tried to associate me with the Priory Church at Leominster, as an honorary member of their clergy team. This I rejected out of hand. I had had nearly three years filling a 'split' post, and I wanted now to concentrate on the job in hand; after all, I had served as a 'parish' priest, as both man and boy, for some twenty-one years. Eventually, a house was found for us off the A49 at Wistanstow, just north of Craven Arms. It happened to be a redundant archdeacon's house in a small village parish, a community which uniquely housed the Rectory (where we were to be billeted), an obsolete Vicarage (which had been converted into flats) and a Parsonage, occupied by the resident parish priest. The Rectory, which had formerly served as home to the archdeacon of Ludlow, was currently being lived in by Bishop Mark Wood, an assistant Bishop of Hereford, who was at the point of retirement.

A moment of embarrassment presented itself on the occasion of my official 'licensing' – a ceremony which took place during a meeting of Diocesan Synod. The subject for discussion at that synod was the contentious question of the ordination of women. During the synod, we were all invited to play a sort of ecclesiastical 'musical chairs', and re-seat ourselves next but one to the person next to us. My wife found herself sitting next to the Diocesan Bishop. Whilst talking to my 'new' companion, I kept an ear open to the discussion between the Bishop and my wife. Suddenly I was horrified to hear her recount the occasion in my former parish, when I had 'con-celebrated' a Communion Service with the Revd. Joyce Bennett the CMS missionary, and one of the Anglican Communion's first ordained women priests. Fortunately I was able to interject, "Not *con*-celebrated darling – it was only a shared Communion service!" I think I got away with it.

Within weeks we had settled into our new home, and I found myself, for the next three years, commuting up and down the A49, from Ross-on-Wye in the south to Shrewsbury in the north, and from the West Midlands, bordered by Bridgnorth, Ledbury and Tenbury Wells in the east to all the remote villages to the west on the edge of the Welsh Marches

Appreciating the problems

My brief was simple and two-fold: to encourage realistic levels of giving among the clergy and parishioners of the parishes of the diocese, and to 'rescue' those parishes which had got themselves into serious financial difficulties, by offering them a series of simple management techniques. Or so I thought. Up until then I had been dealing with urban, business-like men and women, who understood the ways, and finances, of the world. Rural understanding of sacrificial giving was still based on the principle of 'the sixpence on the plate or in the bag on those (few) occasions when you attend!'

Added to this, many of the diocesan parish clergy were not what you would describe as 'grass-roots' parsons, trained after leaving college or university, and who had spent their formative clerical years sitting at the feet of wise and learned incumbents. No, they were, what I came to describe as 'Johnny come lately' men ordained after a life-time in some other trade or profession - many of them ex-teachers – who had very rigid ideas about the Church of England, whose traditional view of 'Anglicanism' was first formed in the chapels of their former public schools. Their liturgical experience went not much further than school 1662 Matins and Evensong, and their knowledge of 20th century hymnody had been arrested at the time of the English Hymnal and 'Hymns Ancient and Modern' Standard Version.. Any awareness of the 20th Century Church Light Music Group, Mission Praise and experimental liturgies was almost non-existent.

Add to this the mentality that, in their opinion, teaching on the subject of Christian giving was not the responsibility of the parish parson, and you ended up with a moribund, stick-in-the-mud, traditional group of men (and later women) whose prime motivation appeared to be 'handle-turning', and not upsetting, but rather maintaining the status quo. Many of the clergy were totally unable to read or understand an annual Statement of Accounts; add to this the convoluted ways in which elderly parish Treasurers presented their Annual PCC Accounts and you had a recipe for total financial disaster. This fact was to prove disastrous within a few years in one rural parish, in which the PCC Treasurer, a well liked and well respected member of the community, who had served the Church for years, finally swindled the PCC out of thousands of pounds, simply because his Accounts were never questioned at the Annual Meeting. He presented the details verbally to the meeting, and he had over several years, forged the signature of a churchwarden in presenting cheques which he then used for his own purposes. This situation obtained for several years, until eventually, when the bank started asking questions about the PCC overdraft, the matter came to light. Before charges could be brought, the gentleman in question committed suicide.

I was continually encouraging parishes to ensure that no PCC cheques were pre-signed in advance, and that all cheques needed to be signed by at least two out of three authorised signatories; I well remember the occasion when I put these principles to one PCC meeting, whereupon the Treasurer, in a state of high indignation announced, "If the Rector is going to expect me to get someone else to counter-sign my cheques, I shall take it as a personal slight against my integrity. If this is the wish of the meeting, then I shall resign as Treasurer, forthwith!"

Discovering the differences in a rural community
Country folk, as I was soon to learn, were simple folk, with very primitive ideas about money, banks, savings and the keeping of accounts. Two stories told me by my archdeacon illustrate this point. On one occasion, he had been asked to celebrate the Holy Communion at a remote village church. After the service, the Treasurer asked him how much he was owed for the communion bread and wine he had brought with him for the service. He replied that he did not require reimbursement, but the Treasurer insisted. "Take whatever it has cost you, out of the parish chest" he was instructed. Upon questioning the system by which loose change was kept in an unlocked parish chest from year end to year end, he was informed: "We put all our collection money in the chest, Sunday by Sunday. Any expenses are taken out as and when – for mower petrol, communion needs, festival flowers and so on. At the end of the year, we count up what is left over, and measuring it against the remaining amount for the previous year, that then tells us whether we have made a profit or loss over the twelve-month."

On another occasion, a rural farmer had travelled into town, and ordered a new tractor with all its fittings and implements. He told the agricultural dealer that he would pay (the considerable sum) upon delivery the following week. On the day the new machinery was delivered, the farmer and the dealer were completing the paperwork, and on being told the final amount due, the farmer asked leave of the dealer, to 'pop upstairs for a moment'. He re-appeared after a short while carrying three large sacks. "I reckon that should cover it" he explained…the sacks were full of five, ten and twenty pound notes! Not only did the farmer not have a bank account, he kept his life savings in paper money in his bedroom – at the regular risk of both fire and thieves!

My work in the diocese took me to parishes large and small, some well motivated, others in a state of financial chaos. At one small rural PCC meeting (to which only four members had turned up) I asked what the financial state of the parish was, and whether I could be given sight of the previous year's accounts. At this point the PCC Treasurer took an empty cigarette packet out of his pocket, tore it apart, and started writing down some figures with a blunt pencil. At the end of about three or four entries he came to his conclusion. "Not counting last Sunday's collection, which I haven't yet collected from the vestry safe, I reckon we have about £22.13p in credit". I found it hard not to show my amazement and dismay!

There were many encouraging occasions as well. Because many incumbents were reluctant to preach on any matters to do with regular, sacrificial giving, I managed to obtain several invitations to preach on a 'Stewardship' Sunday. I enjoyed preaching, and although I never looked for, or expected any form of praise, it was always encouraging when members of the congregation, as they left, thanked me for my thought provoking words. One of my favourite verbal illustrations included the verse from the hymn "Take my life and let it be…" I used to explain that I found it hard to sing the words, "Take my silver and my gold, not a mite would I withhold…" I said that I found that the words stuck in my throat for, if we really *meant* what we were singing, then at this point in the service, half the congregation would be wrenching off their wedding rings, whilst the remainder would be running home to fetch all the family silver!

Computerisation and Desk Top Publishing

It was during this period in my ministry that I finally took the plunge, and with financial assistance from the Diocese, invested in a computer. It was to become a vital tool in my work. I had learnt the intricacies of a typewriter during my army days, so a keyboard presented no difficulties – indeed, throughout my ministry I had been responsible for regular contributions to, and latterly, the editorship of, the monthly parish magazine. Now a whole new world of creative writing, financial analysis and desk-top publishing were at my fingertips. Neither my part-time secretary nor I had any previous experience of computers, but I spent a lot of my spare time facing the challenges my new machine presented, and then passing on my new found knowledge to her, week by week. It wasn't long before I could present my arguments of rising costs and falling income in graphic form to incumbents and PCC's. Not that all of them could read, or even interpret bar-charts, pie-charts and histograms, but some could, and it helped enormously. At the same time, I was now able to produce, very economically, a wide selection of leaflets, bookmarks and posters for both parish and diocesan use.

Although I worked on my own, I had considerable input and companionship from the other clergy in my Rural Deanery. We met once a month for worship and fellowship together in the parishes in our group. I also had a good working relationship with my mentor, Ian Griggs, the recently consecrated Bishop of Ludlow, with whom I 'chewed the fat' once a month, discussing with him my ideas, projects and plans, and taking on board his ideas, caveats and controls.

Apart from my work within the diocese, and my fraternisation with both the clergy and laity of the parishes in which I worked, I also used to travel widely across the length and breadth of the country once or twice a year, attending the annual three and four day conferences organised by the national Stewardship movement. Most of the dioceses at that time had a designated officer responsible for encouraging Christian giving, or concerned with parochial and capital fund-raising, and we enjoyed a fellowship both nationally and within more local, regional groups. Over the twelve years that I worked in Hereford diocese, I travelled to Birmingham, Harlech (twice), Westgate-on-Sea,

Loughborough, Exeter, Scarborough, Cambridge, Wrexham, Weston Super Mare and Newquay. These residential conferences were part fellowship, part study, and part recreation. One notable occasion was our meeting in London Colney in Hertfordshire, attended on our final day by Archbishop George Carey. At the closing Eucharist, I remember, the offertory exceeded £600 – and this from about sixty Stewardship advisers.

A gathering at St. Alban's Diocesan Office of the Group 5 regional Stewardship Advisers with the Rt. Revd. John Taylor, Bishop of St. Albans.

Another unique occasion

It was during one of the Harlech annual conferences that I got myself involved in a unique liturgical exercise. One of the mid-conference recreational visits was a coach journey to a remote Orthodox church, high up in the hills at Blaenau Ffestiniog. The Orthodox Church there served an eclectic congregation of Welsh Orthodox Christians – originally from Poland – a group which had, over the years, been supplemented by Welsh adherents. They had one thing in common – their love of music, and singing. Eastern orthodox liturgies are redolent of the deep masculine harmonies of the Welsh valleys, and although we, as Stewardship advisers made our visit in the interests of widening our ecumenical appreciation, the added bonus was an invitation to attend and share in their evening liturgy. For me, as a priest-adviser, came the added invitation, not only to attend, but to participate in the service.

Following some hastily arranged rehearsals and refreshments, I embarked on another of the highlights of my ministry – sharing with the resident Orthodox priest, Father Deiniol, in the singing of Vespers in four languages – Welsh, Russian, Armenian and English! I travelled back to the conference with the melodies rejoicing in my heart!

Because the parish church of the parish in which we lived was strictly traditional 1662, I looked around for, and found a more forward looking and evangelical church, some ten miles away at Bishop's Castle, and during the time I was in Wistanstow, I joined the church choir. I also ran a successful stewardship programme for them, and enjoyed the fellowship of their choir and congregation. During these three years, I continued my extensive travelling around the diocese, often not returning home until nearly midnight. I particularly remember one foul winter evening, when I had been invited to a tiny rural parish deep in the south of the diocese to address the Parochial Church Council. I drove through snow, sleet, flooded roads and driving rain to get to the Village Hall, and arrived in good time. Eventually, only three of the PCC of some ten or eleven members actually turned up. When I expressed my disappointment, I was politely told that the weather was too bad for them to get to the meeting. I had in fact travelled some fifty-five miles!

On another occasion, this time in the north of the diocese, I arrived at the village hall at the appointed time, and one by one the PCC members arrived – each taking the seat next nearest to the inadequate stove. But no Rector! We waited, and waited, and waited. Eventually, one of the members present took the initiative, and telephoned the Rectory. He was told by the Rector's wife that she hadn't known he had a meeting that night, but that he was asleep in front of the fire; she would wake him and send him on his way directly. Eight minutes later he arrived, and unaware of the message his wife has given us, he then apologised, explaining that he had been at the bedside of a sick parishioner! We hadn't the heart to let him know that we knew otherwise!

An unbelievable preaching occasion
I think the most disturbing preaching visit I ever paid was to the tiny hamlet of Brampton Bryan. The engagement had been arranged with the full consent and invitation of the incumbent, churchwardens and PCC. On the day in question, I arrived in good time (I always did!), to be invited not only to preach, but to take the whole service as apparently the Vicar had forgotten that he was involved in a service elsewhere. Just before the service started, the only churchwarden on duty, the owner of the Manor House in the village, explained that he would be obliged to leave the service in the hymn before the sermon. Foolishly, I commiserated with him, and asked if he had an unavoidable crisis which was demanding his urgent attention. I was flabbergasted by his reply. "We are having a little drinks party at the Manor House at lunch time, which is why my wife hasn't come to church – she is too busy preparing the nibbles. I am needed at home before Matins has finished, in order to prepare the drinks!" I wrote a

strong letter of protest to the incumbent, only to be informed that his churchwarden was an influential character in the village; he was not to be upset, especially as he was a generous contributor to church funds.

A run-in with the Law
One of the perquisites of being both a priest and a diocesan officer was that, just occasionally, a benefit-in-kind came one's way. One of the recreations Jill and I used to enjoy was travelling around the as yet undiscovered areas of the diocese, visiting churches and enjoying the hospitality of the local public houses. Once, in 1989, we found ourselves in the area of the Clee Hill in Shropshire, and within striking distance of a tiny redundant church, set in a hollow of trees, almost obscured from the narrow country road. We set off to investigate. The church we discovered was virtually derelict, the door open, the altar hangings slowly rotting away, the floor and pews covered in bird droppings - altogether a very sorry sight. We had always wanted a pew in the kitchen of our cottage – by this time we had moved from the rectory at Wistanstow to our own house between Bromyard and Hereford. So, I boldly asked the diocesan officer responsible for 'estates and redundant churches' whether I might buy one of the redundant pews from the church. He explained that eventually all the furniture would be taken into store, but that if we really wanted one, we could help ourselves and have one for free; luckily I asked for, and obtained a 'letter of authority'.

About a fortnight to three weeks later, on a weekend when Jill and I had a free day, we set off for the Clee Hill to collect our pew. The church lay at the bottom of a quite steep slope, some two fields from the road. There was a path, and two stiles to negotiate between the car and the church, so we set off on our journey of reclamation. We struggled up the narrow path, loaded down with the pew and the two pew ends. Unknown to us, we had attracted the interest of a farmer's wife in a house within sight of both church and car. As we finally arrived at the car, breathing hard, we were met by a police constable in a Panda Car. Although a little shaken, I was relieved to remember that I had with me the 'letter of authority', which I presented to him. He appeared to be convinced with my explanation, but whist we were negotiating, he was joined by a Motorway Police Patrol car, which had also been summoned to the 'crime scene' by their control centre. The driver of this car, unlike his rustic colleague, was not so easily convinced. But with a little diplomatic negotiation, and the production of my various 'proofs of identity', we finally convinced him of our provenance, and were sent on our way. I believe that my expression of bewilderment and innocent protestations went a long way to settle the outcome.

My life was not without recreational diversions as well. Not only did I get involved in the choir at Bishop's Castle, but when we moved down south to Felton, near Bromyard, I joined an 'ad hoc' eclectic choir at Bromyard church, to share in a broadcast of the BBC's 'Sunday Half Hour'.

Following my involvement with the two Jimmy Owens' evangelical musicals

'Come Together' and 'If my People' whilst at Twyford, I was delighted when a local entrepreneur in Hereford decided to stage a presentation of the more recent work from the pen of a similar 20th century evangelical author, Graham Kendrick. The choir was made up of singers from nearly all the local Christian churches in Hereford and its environs, including Free Church Evangelicals and Roman Catholics. It was a good, ecumenical and interdenominational experience, with several presentations on the fringes of the diocese, and the main event taking place at the Hereford United Football ground. In the event, the 'warm up' events were the more successful, being in smaller, more intimate venues. At the football ground, the vast open spaces paid testimony to the lack of support; the massed choirs were side-lined by the imported Graham Kendrick choir, who were the only singers privileged to have their own microphones, whilst we in the choir were relegated to the back of the south end stand, out of sight (and almost 'out of sound') of the few hundred congregation. However, as a spin off benefit, the whole exercise did a lot for inter-church relationships and. ecumenical co-operation.

Extra-Mural worship
During my stewardship ministry, although declining from taking regular services in nearby churches (the danger was always that once I started that practice, I would be unable to refuse any requests), I did help out at my local church and parish. By co-incidence, just after my wife and I had moved down to Felton, the Vicar of the church I had attended at Bishop's Castle moved down to Tupsley on the outskirts of Hereford city. It was a natural decision, therefore, to pledge allegiance to his new church, a congregation with which we have been involved ever since. I was able to help by taking services for him on the occasions when he was unexpectedly away or on holiday, and my most recent memory was being asked, at the very last minute, to take the Midnight service on Christmas Eve at the sister church at Hampton Bishop when the curate's wife was rushed into hospital to give birth to her baby. An appropriate occasion indeed!

In addition, I got involved with a small, evangelical community Free church near Bodenham; once a year I was invited to take their Sunday morning service, and they always seemed very appreciative of my ministrations.

And so the years passed, and my retirement drew near. Unlike a parish priest, who upon transfer or retirement would be the focus of a farewell or retirement party, as a diocesan officer with a minimum of such support, I decided on a select retirement party, held at our cottage. Those invited would have to be few in number, as the rooms of our cottage could only accommodate a handful of guests. So I invited the Diocesan Financial Secretary, with whom I had closely worked for the previous twelve years, and his secretary, who had provided me with statistical information year on year. I also invited my mentor, the Bishop of Ludlow, and my diocesan, the Bishop of Hereford.

In addition, I invited my 'Support Group', with whom I had met on a quarterly basis and who acted as a 'watchdog' on my plans, and curbed some of my wilder enthusiasms, and 'reined me in'. Jill had come up trumps with appropriate nibbles, and I had laid on a variety of liquid refreshment, bearing in mind the reluctance of some, under stricter drink/drive regulations, to imbibe and then drive home. I received few replies to my invitations, nor did I receive a reply from the diocesan bishop; however, at 6.00 p.m. on the evening of the party, I received a telephone call from his wife, apologising on his behalf for not having replied, and asking whether he could come after all! In the event, he came, and all those present spent a happy evening sharing anecdotes and experiences, including some stories which, until then, I had felt unable to share!

In the office at Crozen Cottage, Burley Gate, Hereford, catching up on some paperwork.

At a presentation in Birmingham by the National Blood Transfusion Service

The dedication at the National Aboretum, Alrewas in 2005 of the memorial to the 11ᵗʰ Hussars [PAO].

Chapter 15

CONCLUSION

This marked the end of my lifetime of ministry – thirty eight years as Curate, Priest-in-charge, Vicar, Rector and Christian Stewardship Adviser. I had suffered bad times – and had enjoyed some very good times – but upon reflection, I had had a very rewarding and satisfying ministry. I had been guilty of many 'clerical errors', but I wouldn't have changed any of it for the world.

If I were to dedicate this book to anyone, it would be to the 'unsung heroes of the church', those clergy who, unrecognised and unrewarded, have gone about their tasks with integrity, not counting either financial gain nor seeking the reward and praises of their fellow men, but serving their Lord sacrificially with love and devotion, and to all the lay people who had supported me throughout my ministry.

If it is not too irreligious of me to end these thoughts and memories with a quote from the scriptures, I can think of no more fitting verse – a particular favourite of mine – with which to draw these recollections and reminiscences to an end, than that from the Gospel of St. John: [21.25]

"There are many other things... ...which, if they were to be written down, I suppose that even the world itself could not contain the books that could be written. Amen"

Printed in the United Kingdom
by Lightning Source UK Ltd.
107537UKS00001B/262-321